The Kept Girl

The Kept Girl

by Kim Cooper

18 January 2015
For Doug & Karen
with all my best
from Kim Cooper

Esotouric Ink

Esotouric Ink
P.O. Box 31227
Los Angeles, CA 90031
www.esotouric.com

ISBN #: 978-0-9910494-0-0

Cover art / design: Paul Rogers
Book design: Richard Schave

Printed and bound in the United States of America

First printing
1   3   5   7   9   10   8   6   4   2

For Richard

The Kept Girl

by Kim Cooper

Advance praise

"Kim Cooper is the perfect Virgil to 1929 Los Angeles, a city that was both a paradise and an inferno. Her knowledge of the city that was is unparalleled, her imagination unnerving. The real-life characters and crimes that would give birth to the pulp fiction of the 1930s and the film noir of the 1940s can all be found here. Aficionados of noir Los Angeles will read *The Kept Girl* with fascination and with growing horror as the terrible crime at its core is revealed."– John Buntin, author of *L.A. Noir*

"Nervy, bold, and shot through with a deep sense of Los Angeles history—the kind that feels practically tactile, as all the best noir narratives do—*The Kept Girl* is a delightful addition to this city's literature. The effortlessness with which it borrows against the Chandler tradition while at the same time retaining its unique intelligence and slyly contemporary flavor is just plain stunning. I can't commend it highly enough."– Matthew Specktor, author of *American Dream Machine*

"Holy cats, this woman can write! *The Kept Girl* evokes 1920s Los Angeles in general and especially Raymond Chandler magnificently, without ever stooping to mere ventriloquism. It abounds in grace notes, snappy character sketches and, yes, similes that keep their dignity even in the presence of the master... Cooper is the real thing... like Chandler, she writes rings around most of what New York is turning out."
– David Kipen, editor of *The WPA Guide to Los Angeles*

Acknowledgments

This book would not exist in its present form if not for certain serendipities and notable generosities.

My great thanks to the Subscribers to "The Kept Girl," who believed in the book before it went to press, and weren't deterred by the sinister precedents that inspired it.

My thanks to Rick Baudé, for graciously sharing his own research into the Great Eleven cult, including scans of scarce publications leading up to the unpublished Sixth Seal, as well as family lore about the group.

Thanks to the late Dorothy Fisher, whose memories of working as Raymond Chandler's secretary at Paramount Studios helped inform his personality, particularly his inter-actions with women.

Thank you, Loren Latker and Frank McShane, for careful research into Chandler's life and affinities.

Thanks to my Esotouric crime bus colleagues Joan Renner and Chinta Cooper, as well as the gentle riders in our care, for listening and responding as I refined the telling of the Willa Rhoads mystery over six Wild Wild West Side tours between 2008 and 2010.

Thank you, Mike Fratantoni, for insights into law enforcement structure and investigations in the 1920s.

Thanks to Gordon Pattison and Nathan Marsak, for helping bring old Bunker Hill and its people to life.

Thanks to Paul Rogers, for the jazziest cover art a period mystery could ask for, and to Phil Goldwhite and Richard Nash for technical assistance above and beyond.

Thanks, Josh Glenn, Denise Hamilton, Victoria Prinz, Matthew Specktor and Ruth Waytz, for careful reading and valuable suggestions.

Finally, my deepest gratitude to Lynn Peril, for the gift of Thomas H. James' scarce self-published pamphlet, which showed him to be a very likely model for Chandler's white knight detective Philip Marlowe and inspired a new way of telling the story of those caught up in the madness of the Great Eleven.

By way of an introduction

The story you are about to read is fiction, but nearly every person, place and incident described is real.

There actually was a cult of angel worshippers in 1920s Los Angeles, who squeezed a rich man's nephew dry while promising him access to wealth unimagined. The writer Raymond Chandler, though he was then still an oil executive, truly was one heartbeat away from their weird operation.

And an idealistic young policeman, his courage and foolishness inevitably reminiscent of Philip Marlowe's, walked his beat at the busiest intersection in Downtown Los Angeles, two blocks east of Chandler's office.

The crimes described are real crimes, for the least of which their perpetrators stood trial.

My sources include period newspapers and court pleadings, rare privately-printed pamphlets, self-published memoirs, period maps and photographs, and perhaps a touch of hoodoo.

These passionate people and their beautiful city deserve to be remembered, for all of them are dust today.

This is what happened.

One

I woke up sour-mouthed in Muriel's room at the Mayfair to the sound of vacuuming in the hall. It had to be after 9, but there wasn't sense in rushing. Nobody expected a vice president before 11, although I tried to give the impression of having just stepped out of the office for a quick errand whenever I did stroll in.

It was late summer, 1929, and the money was shoaled up all around us, warm and seemingly infinite as sand on Venice Beach. Old man Dabney's luck with the drill and talent for cultivating friends in local government and the courts had given everyone at Dabney Oil space to breathe. The world was generous, and we were her favored sons. Most of my fellow executives followed the same loose schedule: newspapers read over the desk, a little dictation, a steam and then lunch across the street at the Athletic Club, bridge after.

1

I played bridge, too, but just for an hour, when the stakes were reasonable. Games ended, my colleagues might move upstairs for a massage, or a swim if they were feeling frisky. My pleasure was to take the air.

Los Angeles had grown up around me into a loose-limbed teenager, tall and jittery. To the sleepy, slightly sleazy grove-man's village that I'd settled in fresh from failing to find an English foothold had come oil and real estate speculation, motion pictures and tourism, dream makers and sharpies.

And people—so many new faces every year. Swinging my stick above the lurid terrazzo cartoons that stood in for sidewalks along Broadway, I passed shop windows bursting with bright fashions, while the prettiest women in the world strolled by with that peculiarly brisk gait that I'd never seen anywhere else.

The Art Deco was in fashion, and everywhere the eye was caught by zigzagging chevrons of gold, silver, crimson or black. They were pressed into clay panels being applied to the new buildings along Hill Street, crystalline structures with sharp crests that blocked the sun. You saw them beneath the knees of the women, bright bands of color against the plain crepe of their day dresses, or printed on the shopping bags heaped in the backs of open cars where hulking drivers sat and smoked in the sun. The style denoted energy and action, abstraction, haste. Ours was a city on fire with

2

becoming, the suburbs reaching farther from the core by the week.

I had friends all over Los Angeles. My barber was Castilian, a real Catholic gentleman. He talked about the impossibility of women while he scraped the morning's film from my cheeks, then bundled me up mute in hot towels scented with orange water. My feet on metal stirrups made me feel very small and young, just so long as the towels stayed on.

Inside the Alexandria, the boy at the coffee counter would slop a little gin in the cup if you left two dimes on top of your paper napkin, and I did on days when the stale darkness of a speak was more than I could bear. Blind Mario mixed up my tobacco behind a tall wooden stand, so I would hear but not see the different leaves blending together on the scale before he packed the pouch. Sometimes I'd close my eyes in his shop, and wonder how it would be to navigate one's life without so essential a sense. I imagined that the smells of his small shop and those brought in on his customers' bodies told him everything he needed to know about the world.

I liked to make new friends. The hotels, bus and train stations were good places to look for the signs. Nervously tapping feet in little slippers too pale for our dirty streets. Fingers twisting together over a pair of gloves. Eyes that found the clock too often, but never seemed to note the time.

3

Some of these fair creatures would be swept up by their people as I watched, but if ten minutes passed after I first noticed a stray, I considered it my English duty to inquire as to the state of her constitution. For if I didn't help her, some wolf surely would.

Today's rescue was a near child from Colorado Springs, a high colored blonde with an overbite and a dress two inches the wrong side of à la mode, who was sitting right at the edge of the longest bench at the bus station. She wanted, of course, to go to Hollywood and make big eyes in motion pictures. As we spoke I saw she had a chance, so I shelved the secretarial school line which sometimes applied.

I had a pretty good lecture on what a smart girl might expect from the nascent industry, the proper ways to go about supporting herself as she awaited discovery, how the Central Casting office functioned, where to find smart shoes at last season's prices.

I played down the warnings, since playing them up seemed to scare these hopefuls into sullen silence. More effective was a throwaway suggestion that she was, of course, sophisticated enough to recognize that there were, as in any business, certain self-important boobs who would waste her time. But only, of course, if she let them.

When I put her on a streetcar bound for a reasonably priced women's-only residence in Crown Hill, she rewarded

4

me with a smile too big and too sincere to last long in Los Angeles, and I set off for the office with renewed energy. I might get a bit of work done yet.

The old man's nephew came into the office around 3 p.m. Such an arrival wasn't especially unusual. Five or six days a month, he'd roll in dressed in that ridiculous après-tennis wardrobe and hole up in the big suite they kept for him at the back of the floor. Years on, I still wasn't clear on what he did there. Sometimes you'd hear the thwack of a golf club against a fresh ball, and there were afternoons when he kept the switchboard operator busy connecting calls and the prettier secretaries took dictation. Dabney Oil pumped on regardless of his shallow efforts, pouring money into the firm so I could spend my own afternoons in idle wanderings around the neighborhood and he could never wear the same socks twice.

It was hot out and I felt a little fuzzy. Muriel, ever anticipatory, had made up the daybed behind my desk. That meant my left ear was close to the old man's wall when his nephew let out that weird howl, then commenced to sob.

The sound of a man crying hysterically is repulsive, and, I discovered, sobering. I was at my desk skimming the mail when the old man came in a few minutes later to ask me to join him next door, where his brother's son was still audibly gulping.

5

The heavy door closed behind us like a jug, and although I kept my own office dim, it still took my eyes a moment to adjust to the symphony of brown velvet drapery, green leather, dark wood and hammered copper that made up the old man's lair. I took my usual seat by the shrouded window, where I liked to play with the slick woven tassel that was only tugged late at night when the cleaning crew came in to swab otherwise untouched surfaces and empty the waste bin.

The nephew looked small in a wing chair facing the wide desk, and when he saw me he rammed his long, wet nose into a filmy hankie and pantomimed an abrupt nasal excavation. When he looked up again, he was pretty well presentable. I was impressed at how he'd pulled himself together, but then it wouldn't do have the help see you flopping like a perch.

The big fish spoke. "Clifford, you know Ray Chandler. He's one of my best men, and I want you to tell him everything that you've told me."

"But, uncle—"

"But, nothing. You want my help and you'll take his, and be glad of it. So shut up!" He gurgled, with that peculiar noise that rich men made when briefly challenged. "Ray, it appears that my nephew has found himself in something of a cash shortage, via certain unorthodox investments. Nothing that you can't untangle, my boy. Clifford is going to tell you all about it, and then you're to spend the next—ah, let's say week—locating as much of the missing assets as you're able, and determining if any fraud has been perpetrated against this lad. I want to know what's happened before I make good on any losses, and if there's a crime that's been perpetrated, perhaps District Attorney Fitts would like to know it."

Clifford Dabney, hunched in the big green chair, looked himself a bit green at the direction his uncle's instructions were taking, but said nothing. The old man was on a roll.

"This won't be the first time and I fear it won't be the last I have to bail young Dabney out, but I swore to his mother I'd see that he was ever safe and well. It's not so very much money he's lost, since I never give him much to lose. How much this time, boy?"

"$40,000, uncle. Over several years, though. Not all at once like that time in Vienna."

"Ray will find it. Now tell him about this ugly old woman who swindled you like the idiot child you are."

The nephew made a dive for his nose rag, and for a long moment the only sound in the room was the wheeze of sobs swallowed in his chest. He made me sick, but I had my position to think of. Today the old man was gnawing at Clifford's manhood, but tomorrow it could easily be mine.

Standing, I suggested he follow me into my office, where he might find the air a little fresher, and we could get down

7

to the business at hand. He came wordlessly, grateful for the chance to get away from his tormentor. Just before shutting the big door, I nodded briskly at the old man, and he returned the gesture. He liked to believe I had rare gifts of intuition and persuasion, and I saw no reason to dissuade him of these fantasies.

The first thing I did was to call for Muriel, without whom nothing of any consequence could be done. And when she came, I asked for coffee. Fifteen minutes later, the three of us were huddled round my desk like old friends, and young Dabney, who was well past thirty, fading fast and probably ought to ease the mauve slacks from his wardrobe, had tucked his slimy tissue out of sight. I later discovered it under the pillow on my daybed. We talked in loose circles about the Ventura wells—a safe topic of conversation since the collapse of old man Gosnell's fraud suit some months before—and the new modernist chairs in the conference room, but when I got down to business and Muriel flipped open her stenographer's pad, he turned vague.

"There really isn't much I can tell you, Chandler. It was a publishing venture, and you know how tricky those things are."

"Are they so tricky?"

"Well, this one was. For one thing, the work I was underwriting was a series, and the writers—well, let's just say they had trouble keeping to a deadline. Then, too, it was all leading up to something quite special, which was not for public consumption. But we never quite got there, did we? And without that last volume, I'm afraid all I put into it is wasted."

He sighed. "It's funny. While we were working together it all seemed so important, but when I told May and Ruth that I didn't have the money for the next-to-last pamphlet–" he trailed off and slumped.

"They didn't have any further use for you?"

"That's right. Nor me for them. I turned off the money, they turned off the charm, and it all seemed sort of dead, all at once. Listen, Chandler—you know this business. My uncle's no great genius, but to hear him tell it you'd think he personally charted the paths of those oil fields and forged every under-reamer bit himself. He was born at the right time and had the right friends to make a killing—something he lords over all of us little mice who eat at his table."

He looked to me for validation. I made a face that could be read as agreement, but that he could never quote me on.

He wasn't finished. "Damn California! This state's made monsters of mere merchants, smug little men from the middle west who think they're kings. But I guess they are kings. All I wanted was to find my own way in the world, bring some wealth to my own table. But it seems like I just fell for a con game, like the idiot he thinks I am."

9

"This May and Ruth were—?"

"The mother and the daughter. Very interesting women. Ruth is beautiful, but it's May who can captivate. They're spiritually enlightened, and I have to admit, some of their ideas do make sense, even now. My wife and I were drawn into the fold, and we enjoyed the sense of community, and the working together towards a greater good. My god, we spent five years with them. We thought they were our friends!"

"And the wealth you mentioned?"

"Oh, I expect it will sound crazy to you. But you see, the angel Gabriel spoke to them—about the sin of Noah, and the secret stolen by his son, Ham—Ham, who was made black by his sins. You know, of course, that there are a great many diamonds in Africa. That's no coincidence. Ham knew where to settle, even if he lacked the technology to drill in Bible days. That was Noah's secret, though: how to read the stars to find the mineral wealth within the earth. And that was what we were waiting for the angel Gabriel to reveal."

He looked me straight on. "Do you think I'm foolish?"

I did, but I also found him sympathetic. I'd been on the wrong side of his uncle's temper often enough to see how the fantasy of controlling wealth untold would be delicious.

"Maybe a bit foolish. But California doesn't just make merchants into kings, it also makes criminals into artists. The best in the world work here, and if you fell for them, they must have been very good at what they do."

10

"Hmmph. That doesn't make me feel any less foolish, but maybe with time it will. In any case, I don't expect you'll find much, but humor the old man, and do try not to make me look like too much of a dolt. While you're out shaking carpets, I think I'll check in for a rest someplace nice. If you've got questions, call the house and Alice will know where to find me."

"Hold on, old man. Give me something to go on. I don't even know these ladies' complete names."

He excused himself and trotted off towards his office, leaving my door ajar. When he returned, he slid a slim, black hardbound case, embossed in gold capitals, The Branch: Headstone Of The Corner, across my desk.

"You'll find enough to keep you busy in the corporation minutes. Anything not accounted for, well, just say we spent it on the iceman." His laugh was a dry cough, then he was gone in a cottontail flash of linen.

So much for my own gentleman's hours. It wasn't often that the old man gave me something to do, but when he did there'd be no rest until I could slide a reasonably thorough report under his door.

I must have looked defeated, because Muriel pressed her cup into my hands and whispered, "Drink up, darling. Brain food." The coffee was bitter, and I choked it down.

An hour later, having split the file into halves, we'd learned that the secretary of The Branch had a gift for taking notes which, while ostensibly written in the English language and broken into paragraphs, conveyed a bare minimum of factual information. We had a few surnames and first initials of officers in addition to our own Mr. Dabney and his wife Alice, a smudged notary stamp from an office in far rural Chatsworth, and headaches from skimming such incongruous gobbledygook as "Can a tree sin? There is no evil in your furniture."

I slid down in my chair until my feet hit the stretcher on the far side.

Muriel said, "I could telephone Chatsworth, try to find this notary Jones, or Jakes, or Janes."

I put my head down on the desk.

"Maybe this Mrs. M. O. Blackburn, President, is in the telephone book. M. is for May, of course. O. may be a maiden name, or a first husband."

I groaned.

"Oh, come on, Ray. It can't be that difficult to track the activities of an idiot like Dabney. He's too stupid to cover his tracks, even if his partners did."

"Easy for you to say. You're used to working all day."

But she was right. And I knew just the man to sniff out Dabney's trail, along with any money that remained.

Two

Leaving Muriel to type up her notes, I slipped out through the tall, cool lobby and into the late afternoon's stream. The lady shoppers had abandoned the boulevards for tea rooms, and the first of the evening's sailors were spread like grains of salt among the businessmen and idlers. Approaching Broadway, the crowds grew thicker, some turning north towards the Subway Terminal, others pouring west from the Pacific Electric station. On the corner, a show was letting out of the State.

I stood still, savoring the sun on my neck and the babble of conversation swirling by. My gaze made a slow survey of the intersection before resting on Tom, solid in his blue serge uniform and white peaked cap. He was holding one gloved palm out to ward off the traffic and using a whistle to conduct a clot of pedestrians to move a little quicker in his wake. The sound was eloquent, and impossible to ignore. The surge of the city flowed a little smoother here, its natural chaos tamed by one man's will.

Tom James was a useful fellow to know, assuming you didn't get on his bad side. He'd started out as cop and risen quickly to Police Commission investigator, but proved to be a little too skilled at investigating, and frankly awful at keeping his mouth shut. Principles will get you killed in some municipalities, but Tom's foster mother was connected to most of the charitably-minded matrons in the Blue Book, so his superiors bounced him back down the ladder into grunt police work in hopes, still as yet unrealized, of boring him into retirement.

I'd met him first right here, on the Broadway beat. Helping people across the street wasn't really one of his duties, but he liked the exercise and the chance to make quick conversation a hundred times a day. Some of the things he said worried me, but Tom's notion was that if everyone in town knew him as a clean cop who liked to rail against corruption and name names, they wouldn't dare do anything to him.

So far, he was right.

Tom did one circuit around the intersection clockwise, then turned on his heel and started back the other way. I imagined he didn't see me as I fell into stride just behind him on his return trip, but when I spoke he picked up the thread as if we'd been conversing for hours.

"I hear the mayor's got his hands in some pretty dirty pies, officer."

"Well, some folks do say that Los Angeles is not exactly the white spot by which she calls herself. Not that a lowly old beat cop would know anything about that. Hello, Ray. To what do I owe the pleasure?"

"Can't a fellow take an afternoon constitutional to enjoy a visit with his favorite civil servant?"

"Naturally, but what are you doing downtown at such an hour? I'd expect you to be home in your dressing gown with your feet up, a fat old executive like you. Hang on there. Miss, wait please! Your turn is coming!"

"When do you get off, Tom? I've got a problem, and it could be a bit of work for you. Can we talk somewhere?"

"I can come see you this evening, about 7. At your house?"

"No, come to the Mayfair."

"Oh, to Muriel's place?"

"Room 812. We'll order up some dinner. Thanks, friend. Watch out for those crooked captains."

Later, big hands folded beneath his chin, a glass of seltzer beside him, Tom tried to convince me I didn't need a detective at all.

"This is boy's work. Run down a few old addresses, talk to the neighbors, check property records, bribe a couple of bank clerks. Dabney practically gave it to you already."

"Boy's work for you, maybe. I couldn't possibly bribe a bank clerk without laughing. They'd take it for a robbery and start shooting at me. Come on, we both know you miss detective work. And I'll pay you. Say yes."

Muriel got up and touched his shoulder, "Please, Tom. Ray might lose his job if this isn't done right. It's a lot of money's gone missing, and the old man expects a full report. We do need your help."

"All right, all right—I'll help you. I won't do everything, but I'll do the hard business and make sure neither of you gets in deeper than is safe. We'll find out what young Master Dabney's squandered his inheritance on, where the money's gone and who took it off him. But you're not going to pay me. I'm your friend. You can feed me, but you can't pay me."

"Let's start with dessert," said Muriel, passing a sheath of papers.

"What's this? Hmm, phone logs?"

"That's right. There were three occasions over the past four years when Dabney was in the office and I covered the switchboard. These are all the calls that he made out, and the one call that came in for him on those dates. I'm afraid I didn't stay on the line after the calls were connected. But it's something, no?"

"Memory girl," I sang. "Isn't she marvelous? I don't know how she does it, but any time there are numbers, she's a magician. You should see her with canceled checks when we're balancing the books."

Muriel flushed. "Stop it, Ray. I can't help the way my mind works. Is this helpful, Tom? Can you track the people at the other end?"

"Oh, easily. I'll just go down to headquarters and scan the reverse directories. Between these and the incorporation papers, there are plenty of doors to try."

"So we'll start tomorrow?"

"I'll see there's something for you to do tomorrow. I'm digging in tonight. Now get some rest. I want to see you both at Dabney Oil at 8 o'clock, no excuses!"

Bunker Hill hunkered above the city like a dyspeptic's dream of childhood.

Its broad boulevards were striped with once handsome houses gone gray with neglect: broken shutters, missing gingerbread, open windows flying the mismatched curtains of each lodger's cheap taste. Scattered among them, still, a few fine houses retained some natural elegance, but the beige hulks of shadowy cheap hotels spoiled the vista and the pong of cat urine rode the breeze.

Tom sat in his car on Grand Avenue, watching for signs of life at 355. It was years since he'd been up on the hill. He remembered a tea party on the back lawn of some hotel, the mothers laughing under sun hats while the children played jungle explorer on the slope that hung over the new city. Most of the places had had show gardens once, but with long neglect they'd given way to impenetrable rats' nests of morning glory and bamboo, and any child venturing into them today would soon emerge scratched, sore and eager to be bathed.

A shadow passed from the front parlor to the hall and he was quick up the path, tapping neat professional knuckles against the glass. The porch light snapped on and a small, aged woman stepped out. She pulled her kimono tight against the night and looked worried. "Is something wrong, officer?"

"Nothing's the matter, ma'am. But did a May Otis Blackburn live here once?"

She stiffened. "That one! And her slut daughter, too. What have those witches done now?"

"That's what I'm trying to find out. Could you tell me about them?"

The lady took him in with tired gray eyes, seemed about to refuse, then shrugged. "Oh, come on in."

She led him into the parlor and gestured to a fine oak armchair which he imagined must have been her father's. Many of these old houses were in the care of spinster daughters who had no choice but to open their homes to strangers, not all of them nice. The heavy furniture, dark paneling and fussy flower paintings spoke of an earlier Los Angeles, where black-suited husbands rode the funicular down the hill to their banks and stores, and the young ladies of the house practiced French and needlepoint, skills which either earned them a husband and a Pasadena club life, or a white elephant of a house and late-night visits from moonlighting policemen.

"Cup of tea? No? Well, I guess I've got nothing better to do than dredge up memories of old lodgers." She settled herself on a rocker beside the fireplace. "What do you want to know?"

"Tell it to me from the beginning, How they came here and what you recall of them. Appearance, behavior. How they came to leave."

She closed her eyes and tucked her knees up sideways in the chair, then spoke slowly, as the memories flowed.

"It was the first season I had to take in boarders, and I thought the best thing would be to split the house and rent the whole upstairs to a family. This house is too big for one person, anyway. I advertised in "The Times" and several families came up to meet me and see the place. I suppose I'm a snob, but none of them seemed right. The children had sticky hands, or I didn't like the father's mustaches. Such a stupid woman. I'm sure any of those families would have been perfectly fine to live with."

19

"It's not easy to make a change in how you run your house, Miss—"

"Loomis. But call me Opal, Officer—?"

"Thomas James. Tom, to you. But you did find boarders?"

"I did. May Otis came, with her daughter Ruth. They fooled me very nicely, and I let them move into my home. Let them sit in this parlor on a Sunday. Oh, we had beautiful silver and enamel candlesticks on this mantle when they came, but you won't see them now. And my mother's best scarf on the piano." She sighed into her chest and pushed a fist against her thigh.

He chucked softly, as to a bird or a small child. It was a sweet sound. It made her smile.

He smiled, too. "Now Opal, tell it to me like you're telling a story about something that happened to another person. Like it was in a book. Bad things may happen, but it doesn't mean you've been bad."

She shook her head. "Please, I'm not naïve, Tom. But I am embarrassed not to have suspected anything was wrong, because absolutely nothing was right with those two. Their story was that they'd come from New York, because Ruth had an introduction to a motion picture studio. This was as a dancer, and she was a dancer all right—but not from New York, and not in the movies. After they were gone the creditors tracked them here, so I know they lived in Oregon some time before Los Angeles. I should have known it, they sounded country. Anyway, May wrote all the time, in the little tower room. Ruth worked down on Main Street, in one of the dance halls. Love Land. I'm not prejudiced against entertainers, but that's practically prostitution. And she was silly enough to tell her customers where she lived, so I'd have to sweep tom cats off my porch plenty of nights."

"Did they pay their rent?"

"Not always on time, but they paid. That was the problem, though. The money came from poor Arthur Osborne, and they treated him like dirt. He used to sit in my kitchen and cry over how Ruth treated him, and the things her mother said. So all in all, they weren't quite what I had in mind when I determined to rent those rooms out. I was ready to ask them to go, too, but they went without being asked."

"When was that?"

"They stopped here at Christmas, 1923, and left in the summer of '24. May told me all her prayers had paid off, and they were moving into a big house of their own."

"Do you know where they went next?"

"They left no forwarding address, but I had the impression they were going west. And with them went some of the nicest things in this house, as I discovered soon enough."

"You don't happen to have a photograph of the ladies, do you?"

"I have one of Ruth."

She crossed the room and rifled in the piano bench, coming up with a glossy print of a curly-haired, cow-eyed teen, her curves draped in lace and long beads.

"You can take it. She signed it to me the night we met. Told me it would be worth a lot when she became a movie star. Her mother looks nothing like her. Plain woman, but she isn't plain when she speaks. She's not attractive, but she's compelling. I don't think any photograph would do May justice."

"You've been a great help, and I thank you. Just one more thing. Where can I find this Osborne, the man who paid their rent?"

"Arthur? You can find him in this house. He was so broken up when Ruth left—you see, she didn't tell him she was going, although they were supposed to be engaged. I felt sorry for him and I let him move into Ruth's bedroom. She'd left her bedding and some clothes, so he just crawled in and cried into her rags, and he never left. He's a nice boy. Works down in Long Beach in the oil fields. It's too late to wake him, but come by before breakfast or some evening after seven. He'll talk to you. Any excuse to talk about Ruth suits Arthur. I don't think he'll ever get over that girl."

Tom sat at the counter of a Main Street donut shop, warm mug cradled in cupped hands.

Outside, the night throbbed with the energy of a thousand passing souls. Cars zoomed by, a neon script buzzed in the window, and he heard shards of laughter and conversation each time the glass door opened. Through a narrow doorway, a black man all in white minded the fry basket, and the quiet waitress sailed the length of the counter on her own lunar time table, catching his eye and topping up his coffee every time it lost an inch. Behind him in a booth, two figures of indeterminate gender bickered in low tones, and on the neon-ringed clock above the register, both hands came together just past 1.

Tom studied the photograph Opal Loomis had given him. It was a professional shot, but the subject lacked the confidence of a true stage performer. Ruth Wieland, Danseuse was printed across the bottom, beneath a photographer's logo, Levy. Across the pale backdrop, large, looping letters in purple ink read "For dear Miss Loomis, with great affection, from Ruth Angeline Wieland." Over the A in Angeline, an angled oval formed a jaunty halo.

Ruth looked to be in her middle teens, still with the fat of youth on her limbs. Her elbows were akimbo and palms pushed together above her head as if in prayer. Egyptian bangles ringed her upper arms, a chain cinched her waist, and she was barefooted. Ruth had the requisite vamp's lips and dramatic eyebrows, a womanly bosom obscured by a twisted length of gauze, and slim hips, but her expression was vapid. The overall impression was of a pretty, stupid thing with an undeniable sexuality not enhanced by the dated pose. Her costume looked homemade and noisy, like a boudoir lampshade packed with meat. He could imagine the swish-swish of beaded strings and the curves revealed as the strings swayed, and wondered what she looked like in street clothes.

Draining his mug, Tom tucked the photo under his arm, nodded to the waitress and stepped outside. Main Street, which never slept, was in full summer bloom and bright as day. Above broad marquees, angular blossoms of bulbs opened and contracted. The crack-crack of a rifle sounded from an open-air shooting gallery, where a skinny Mexican youth was showing off for his compadres. He saw light from the back of Goldie's pawn shop, where no honest business was done at night. The gutter flowed with soapy water and chunks of vomit.

Across the boulevard, an incandescent arrow sign promised GIRLS * 100 * GIRLS * DANCING.

This was the Love Land Ballroom, the taxi dance parlor where Arthur Osborne had discovered Ruth Wieland.

The building was an old three-story brick pile with a narrow entryway. At its end, a heavyset girl napped in a cashier's cage. A whitewashed staircase led up to her right, and he could hear tinny echoes of a dance band above. A hand-lettered sign, flyspecked red with gold outlines, advertised ENTRANCE 50¢—TICKETS 10 / $1—NO MIN.

The taxi dance hall was the lowest rung of romantic possibility, a place for men who couldn't otherwise commune with a woman to buy a stray moment of forged affection. Ten cents a dance, and the dance would be a quick one, the band burning bridges in its race to boil each popular tune down to its jumpy essence.

Upstairs, he knew, the long wall under the open windows would be lined with the lonely and the lame, recent immigrants, old men in suits that smelled of dust, the disfigured and the portly. The prettiest girls were swept up early by eager beavers who bought long rolls of tickets and redeemed each one with a lover's flourish. Those that were left were shared among the customers, suffering stomped toes, grinding embraces, sour breath, hair tonic rashes and the occasional illiterate's love letter smashed into her cleavage.

It was, he mused, a sort of church to the ideal of romantic love, however little of the stuff was actually dispensed there.

Feeling suddenly mean, Tom took a nickel from his pocket and ran it along the grate above the cashier's head. The girl jerked up from her lap with narrow eyes and snapped, "Hey, copper, we're all paid up here. Lemme call the manager, he'll tell you." Tom smirked at her, "That will be fine, ma'am." She sneered back, picked up a phone and screeched "Arnie! Come out here! There's a uniform at the door!"

Ten minutes later, a tall, skinny man in a tight tweed suit came halfway down the stairs, gave Tom a withering look, jerked his neck in a "get up here" gesture and started up again. Tom followed up two flights and down a grimy hall lined with half glass doors, to an open portal on the left labeled Arnold Weiss, Proprietor. Weiss sat with his back to the door, behind a broad desk that was empty save a spindle piled six inches high with pink receipts. The walls were papered with glossy photographs of dancers, and in the corner hulked an old safe decorated with lavender hollyhocks. Tom pulled up a chair and waited. A long beat, and Weiss spun around in his chair and leveled a stare built to wilt.

"I know you, friend. You're that troublemaking cop what got demoted to the Broadway beat. Well, this ain't your beat and you shouldn't oughtta stick your nose into mine. There's nothing here for you. Ask your captain if you want to get bounced some place even lower than Broadway. This is Main Street, kid. So buzz off."

26

Tom yawned. "Spare me the soliloquy, Weiss. This is no shakedown, but I'll take some information if you've got it. I'm on a tail job, private customer."

"Yeah, straight arrow like you, making a few bucks on the side?" Weiss grinned, glad to change tack. There were few things duller than chastising a stupid cop. "That's rich. Shoot, kid. Who's your quarry?"

The photo flipped across the desk. "Do you remember this girl, Ruth Wieland? Danced here maybe five years back?"

Weiss chuckled. "That one I remember. Cuckoo cuckoo. The girls called her Salami—a play on Salome, for this weird business she did with her scarf between dances. Wieland, Wieland—" he leafed through a low file cabinet under the window and pulled a folder free.

"Here she is. Made her debut January 4th, 1924, retired April 15th. Solid performer, when she bothered to come in. Sexy kid, though. Had a couple of regulars who didn't mind the scarf and the swooning. I docked her once for showing up with stains in her pits. Says here she wouldn't dance with Filipinos—but our Asiatic clientele isn't much interested in big, dark girls anyway. Salami, huh? Who'd pay you to look for that nut? Jilted customer?"

"Something like that. So where'd she go from here?"

"Looks like we mailed her last week's wages. 355 South Grand, Bunker Hill. And her name ain't Wieland anymore, it's Rizzio. She's married—or at least she was in '24."

"Thanks, brother."

"Think nothing of it. Always glad to assist a representative of our city in his official duties."

Arthur Osborne was a rabbit-eyed man whose delicate head bobbed awkwardly on brawny shoulders. Dressed in clean khakis, he perched on Opal Loomis' ottoman, peering into the unlit fire. His voice was deep, but uncertain. He was thinking.

"Ruth Wieland is a wonderful girl. She is an artist and an aesthete, with so much to give to the world. She left here to finish her Great Work—her's and her mother's—and I am happy to await her return. I only hope it will be soon."

"You met her at the Love Land?"

"Yes, and I'm not ashamed to say it. Why shouldn't a man go out in search of love? Nobody ever knows where the soul's milk will find him. One can find love in a classroom, on a city bus, in a foreign port, or dancing with a stranger. I danced with many strangers, but when I put my arms around my little Ruthie, I knew in an instant that she was the light of my heart."

"Miss Loomis tells me you supported Miss Wieland and her mother?"

"Gladly. I told Ruth she was wasting herself at that dance hall. She was polluting her impressions with base reality. Main Street is full of darkness, a place where good souls are tested in the furnace of lust and depravity." He laughed. "But I guess I don't have to tell you that, officer! It took hours each time she came back up the hill to shake off the emanations and open up the channel, so she could write again. I helped her, for the sake of her soul and of their work."

"So when she left the dance hall in April, 1924, that was because you'd offered to pay her expenses. Then what happened?"

"It was wonderful. I always knew where Ruthie was, and that she was safe. She and Mother May shut themselves up in the round room for days on end. I brought them delicacies to feed their thoughts, everything they asked me for, and some nights they came downstairs and allowed me to sit and listen as they read from the work. Mother May gave me instruction in the Bible. And Ruth danced for me. We were so happy."

"But then they went away?"

"You have to understand, the channel is very delicate. It will only open for a pure soul in a pure place. Bunker

29

Hill was built for bankers! Mother May explained to me that one day she and Ruth might have to leave, to go some place unsullied where the channel needed them to be, and that I must be brave and patient. That day came sooner than I dreamed. But it's all right. I have a nice room here where I can remember my love, and I know when the Sixth Seal is completed I will see her again. And while I wait, I'm still helping them with the work."

"Helping?"

"Oh yes. I still tithe 25 per cent of my income, every week."

"You call Ruth 'Miss Wieland.' Have you ever known her to be called Mrs. Rizzio?"

"Certainly not. Ruth is a maiden. Someday she'll be Mrs. Osborne."

"What about Clifford Dabney? Have you ever heard that name?"

"Any relation to that oilman Joseph?"

"Nephew. Know him?"

"No. Only know his uncle by reputation. I'm in the field, you know. And I better catch my car if I'm going to keep my job. Hope this has been helpful, officer."

"It was, and thanks for your candor."

"No, thank you. I love to talk about Ruth. Come back and we'll talk some more." Osborne stood and screwed his cap on. "I'll see you out."

"One more thing. When you tithe money, where do you send it? Are they up near Chatsworth now?"

"Chatsworth? I don't think so. Anyway, I don't send it. I give cash to Ward, for them."

"Ward?"

"Ward Blackburn, Mother May's husband. He's on his point at the corner of Western and Wilshire most of the time, so I just swing by after I cash my check. Ward's how I keep in touch with Ruth now. He's sort of an ambassador for the ladies, since they spend so much time indoors, immersed in the work."

"So if I wanted to get a message to Ruth or her mother, I'd talk to Ward? How would I know him?"

Osborne hooted. "You can't miss Ward! He looks just like a Mandarin. If you see a pale little white fellow with long mustaches and fingernails holding onto a coffee can, that's Ward. He'll probably be counting cars. If you see him, tell him I'll be by real soon."

It was nearly 8. Tom left his car on Bunker Hill and walked down to Dabney's office, turning over the night's discoveries in his mind.

Ruth and May were probably still in Los Angeles, or nearby, maybe as far away as Chatsworth. They'd come into some money in spring 1924, enough to rent or buy a home of their own, but not so much that they cut Arthur Osborne off completely. The time frame coincided with Dabney's meeting the women, so it was safe to assume his bank account had had something to do with their move off Bunker Hill. Somewhere along the way, May had taken a husband, who sounded like a screwball, and was based in Los Angeles. Ruth had a husband, too. The women were larcenous enough to snatch Opal Loomis's candlesticks, and charming enough to keep pocketing Arthur's wages in exchange for minimal, second-hand contact.

He could picture round Ruth, arching her back in the beaded costume, and understood the appeal.

Mother May was more elusive. He knew that she was a seductive, ugly woman, but as yet had no clue as to the forms the ugliness or attraction took. He wasn't quite ready to find her. He sensed that she was complicated and dangerous, and wanted to know more before approaching her head on. Assuming she could be located.

Of course, everybody could be located.

Passing Pershing Square on his left, the burble of fountains and morning birdsong caught his ear. An old woman with a guitar hitched up to her neck was standing on a bench, craning for an audience. She caught his eye, strummed a muted chord and waved him over with the neck of her instrument, but Tom just waved back and quickened his pace. He felt exhilarated to be untangling a mystery again, but sore from the long hours watching and questioning. It would be good to put the case back into Ray's hands for the day and get some rest.

At Seventh Street he swung right, through massive columns framing the tall bronze doors of the Bank of Italy. The lobby was cool and dark, suffused with the clean smell of capital. Tellers stood behind wrought iron screens, their edges burnished with gold leaf and flashes of red, green and blue. Above, deep recesses in the wooden ceiling glowed with pigment. The bank was busy, but as if in deference to the chapel-like space, no customer raised his voice above a whisper.

A signpost reading LADIES BANKING—MEZZANINE stood near the wide stair. At the back of the room, a stand of four ornate elevators waited to ferry patrons to the business suites above. Tom stepped into the only open one.

"Your destination, officer?" The dapper attendant was a cripple, perched on his stool beside the big wheel. He was an old man with youthful skin that rarely saw daylight, and the patient demeanor of one whose journey never varied.

"12th floor, Dabney Oil."

If he found anything unusual in a rumpled beat cop asking for a ride to the top, the attendant gave no sign. With two smooth motions he closed the cage and sent the capsule rolling smoothly upward. They passed a moment in discrete silence before Tom was ushered gracefully into a long

33

hall. Each of the wooden office doors led to some division of the Dabney Oil Syndicate; between them glowered portraits of anonymous burghers who'd made their fortunes centuries before, on wheat, slaves, silk or hardwood. The hall was quiet, and he instinctively tried to hush his steps over the rose pink marble path.

Room 1208 was labeled in crisp golden letters: South Basin Oil Co. / R.T. Chandler—Vice President. Muriel ushered him in before his second rap. Ray looked up from behind his desk with a grin.

"Tom! Summer morning in Los Angeles is absolutely glorious. Why didn't anyone tell me? Sit, sit. Muriel, bring tea!"

"I'd rather have coffee, if you've got it. It's been a long night."

"Of course. Coffee all around. And the boy's sending up sandwiches. A long night, and I hope a fruitful one?"

Tom briefed them on his conversations with Opal Loomis, Arnie Weiss and Arthur Osborne.

Ray pressed his palms together, and brought his fingers to his lips. "Interesting. But rather old news, isn't it?"

"At this point, we're still filling in the gaps that tell the story, but I wouldn't be surprised to see us narrow in on the present, and the money, soon enough. I'm going to hand the investigation off to you for the day, get some sleep and work my beat, then we can meet again tonight. Why don't you go down to Wilshire, try to find Ward Blackburn and see if he'll let on where the ladies are staying? And I expect it wouldn't hurt to speak with Dabney's wife. She was in this thing, too, but might not be as cavalier about the loss. Don't tell them anything more than you need to, but try to get them to open up. You're a good listener, it won't be difficult."

"Done and done. Then I'm buying you dinner, Tom. Good Fellows Grotto, 8 o'clock?"

"I'll be there. And have you searched Dabney's office yet? No? Do so. Any correspondence or banking records that seem unusual, bring them tonight."

Ray chuckled. "That's simple. It would be unusual to find any business documents to speak of in young Dabney's office. I'll bring the lot."

"Good day, you two. Good luck."

Ray and Muriel peered through the windshield at an eccentric figure.

Ward Blackburn, for it could only be he, stood on the southeast corner of Western and Wilshire Boulevard, executing a repetitive series of movements. First he bowed almost to the ground, then swept his hands up over his head into an inverted V. He stepped back, opened his arms wide, threw his head back, extended his tongue and grinned up at the sky, his mustaches flicking like cat's whiskers. He did this several times, then fell back on his haunches. His thick gray robe pooled around his feet, and rippled as he bounced on the sidewalk in front of the little house that held a high class real estate office. A few minutes later, he rose and repeated the actions. The flow of pedestrians paid little mind to his activity, for this was Los Angeles, and gurus were thick on the ground and mainly harmless.

"So that's the earthly conduit to the holy ladies. I begin to have a better understanding of young Dabney's proclivities."

"I think he's cute," said Muriel. "More men should wear dresses. It might improve relations between the sexes."

Ray snorted. "Back soon, girlie. Don't let me find you in trousers on my return."

He strolled down the sidewalk, feigning preoccupation with his pocket watch. Nearing the corner, he discovered that Ward wasn't just crouching, he was counting. "83, 84, 85—" At "100" Ward took a peanut from the pocket of his robe and dropped it into a coffee tin. "1, 2, 3, 4—" Against the lamp standard leaned a grubby wooden sign that read THE SEVENTH TRUMPET OF SAN GABRIEL—SECRET OF THE AGES JUST 25¢.

"Secret of the ages, eh? What are you selling, man?"

Ward wheeled, delighted to be addressed, pressed his palms together in a benediction and beamed. As he spoke his first full sentence, Ray recognized that the man was both subnormal, and a true believer.

"Fortunate friend, you have found the truth about life and the world everlasting. The cost is small for a booklet, but the value is great. I'll show you, wait!"

Ward could do nothing casually. He pressed the nut-filled coffee tin into Ray's hands, and with a flourish spread open his robe to reveal a veritable bookshop, interior pockets stocked with rows of slim pamphlets. The open robe also revealed, to Ray's relief, a rather nicely tailored shirt, bow-tie and linen trousers.

"This is Number One, the first of the revelations, so if you're going to start, this is the place to do it. But we have also Number Two, Number Three, Number Five and Four, 25¢ each or the full set for only one dollar."

Ray took the proffered pamphlet, with its amateurish cover drawing of an androgynous angel poking itself in the ear with a wire-thin trumpet. He skimmed the pages, noting long passages of biblical quotations in red, and section headings named for musical notes.

"How interesting. So, you're a Christian?"

"Oh, no. I am a member of the Great Eleven Club. We don't sneer at Christ, but we leave him in the past where he belongs. This is a modern world, friend. We need modern prophets, who understand machines—and science!"

"I quite agree with you. Just look around us. I often ask myself, what could Jesus Christ make of Los Angeles today? So in this club, you meet and study these pamphlets?"

"Yes we do, and we do other things. I, for example, am right now on my point. That means I am doing what I was born to do, right here on Wilshire Boulevard. Would you believe it? Some people have to travel to Jerusalem to find their spiritual home, but not me!"

"Aren't you a lucky fellow? But what does that mean, 'on your point?' Selling books on the corner?"

"Oh no no no, I'm just trying to save your soul now, and I am off my point. On my point is much more fun. It's a sunny day, so today I'm counting the cars. Every hundred cars is one peanut, and if I fill up the coffee tin, I just put one peanut in my trouser pocket and I start all over again."

"That's very scientific, friend. What would you do if it weren't sunny?"

"That's easy. I'd stand right over there under the awning, put my coffee tin out by the curb, and measure the rain-drops."

"Marvelous, simply marvelous. You must feel so ful-filled."

" I do, that's exactly how I feel. Will you take a pamph-let?"

"I shall buy them all. May I give you two dollars, for two sets? I have a friend also in need of enlightenment. He is one of those people who has everything he needs, but nothing that he wants, if you catch my meaning."

"Yes, certainly!" Ward fussed around inside his robes, then handed over the small stack of bound booklets in return for a quarter eagle coin, making change in dimes.

"Thank you so much! So, once my friend and I have read these books, what then?"

"Oh, you can read them, but you won't understand them. To understand, you must attend meetings. You will have dreams to let you know when you're ready, and when you are, come to 640 South Manhattan Place on a Sunday, at three in the afternoon. Three is a significant hour. You are most, most welcome. Bring five dollars!"

"Do you teach the class?"

Ward laughed, a long, hiccupping wheeze that made his whiskers flick like the antennae of a catfish. When it seemed as if the laugh was starting to hurt, he clapped both hands over his mouth, gulped, and collected himself. His answer was less dramatic. "I just listen. Come, maybe you'll meet Mother, and if not, you'll still learn something. You look like you could stand to learn something."

Never one to take offense from an idiot, Ray simply agreed. "I imagine we all could stand to learn something. So it's your mother that teaches the class?"

"Not my mother, Mother. My wife. Mother Manifesting the Heel of God. The May Queen. She has many names, many faces—"

The sharp blast of a car horn interrupted his litany. A newish dark green panel truck waited at the curb across the boulevard, a swarthy young man at the wheel.

Ward grabbed the coffee tin out of Ray's hand, straightened his robe and snatched up the wooden sign, chanting a rushed farewell. "Gotta go now, toodle-oo, see you sometime unless I don't."

He crossed Wilshire, hitched up his skirts and climbed into the cab. The truck took off, heading north.

Ray watched it pull away, noting that the same awkward angel from the pamphlets was painted across the back panel. A ribbon-like rainbow along the bumper was dotted with what looked like musical notation. He squinted but was unable to read the script above the colors.

Turning on his heel to return to the car, he saw Muriel swing a wide left turn into heavy traffic, then speed after the vanishing eccentric. He yelled after her, but she just waved two gloved fingers, gunned the motor and was gone.

Sighing, Ray tucked the neat stack of tracts into his jacket pocket and set off in the same direction. Young Dabney's house was just a few blocks north, and he might as well hear what the lady wife had to say.

Three

Muriel craned her neck over the wheel of the company Hup-mobile, following half a block behind the green truck. She'd impulsively decided to keep driving so long as it stayed in view.

Leaving Los Angeles was simple. From Western, the truck cut left onto Sunset, then right up the Cahuenga grade.

The city fell away, and soon they were just two dots on a busy country highway. Muriel raised her window against the dust. To each side, rows of citrus trees scrolled their illusionary pathways, the pattern broken occasionally by a windbreak of eucalyptus or an old farm house set back in the fields. The air was hot and fragrant with fruit, and fat black bugs smashed against the wind-screen in greasy yellow blotches. Ahead of her, the truck held steady at 45 miles per hour, the silver paint around the angel flashing with every bump. She held the long, powerful car in check. The

41

sun tilted in the sky, and the hulking mountain ranges on each side began to show the colors of a bruise.

At Girard, the truck cut north towards Owensmouth, then left the road at Chatsworth. Muriel slowed and followed, waiting kitty corner as it stopped at a gas station with a restaurant alongside. A tall wooden sign was painted with a cartoon of a tiger devouring a chicken dinner atop a picnic table, while a scantily-clad waitress jumped back in alarm.

The driver stepped out and stretched. He was small and well-built, with curly dark hair worn long. His work clothes showed some attention to his shape, and as he strode back towards the toilets, he bounced on his heels.

The white-overalled attendant came out, spoke briefly to Ward through the passenger window, then pumped some gas, cleaned the windscreen and looked under the hood. The driver returned, conferred with the attendant over the engine, paid, then took the wheel.

Off the highway, Muriel was conscious of her quarry's eyes, and hung further back. The green truck rolled through the town, then turned left onto the Santa Susanna Pass Road. Another truck turned in before she could follow, and she trailed them both through the dusty rise. After a time, the green truck slowed to let the other pass, crept ahead, then made a right on a narrow, gravel-lined road framed with old wooden gates.

Hanging from a chain was a hand-painted oval sign with a stylized silhouette of the familiar angel figure and in black script HARMONY HAMLET → 2 MILES. Pleased, and suddenly ravenous, she turned around and returned to the sign of the hungry tiger.

The lanky attendant, whose name badge said Carl, tended to the car while she strolled back towards the diner. It was, she realized only then, shut up tight, with the first signs of dereliction showing. Down towards the creek, picnic tables were piled high with fallen leaves. She used her thumb to rub a ring in the dirty window and peeped inside. A long steel counter took up the majority of the small front room. Through an archway she saw set tables with dead flowers in wine jugs.

"She cleared out."

Carl had crept up silently behind her. Muriel started at the gravelly voice with its Oklahoma twang, then laughed at herself.

"That so? Shame. It looks like a nice business."

"Oh, it was a nice business, true enough. But not nice enough for her."

"Lady ran it?"

"With her husband. Came out here from Long Beach two summers ago. Did all right. Early breakfast trade for the farmers, picnic dinners for travelers through the day.

43

Did even better once they put a copy of that sign up on the highway. Then about eight months back, he gets sick, so she brings in some help. From Long Beach. Young fellow. Cook."

There was something insinuating in Carl's voice which made the most innocuous phrases sound sinister.

Muriel blurted out, "Don't tell me they killed her husband?"

Carl's laughter blew the cobwebs from the scene. "Good god, no! Woman, you've been seeing too many movies. What happened was she ran the place alone for a couple months, got bored and shut her down. Husband's in a sanitarium in Ventura, she's living close by. Reckon they'll come back if he gets well, unless he's got a better option. Now if it were my place, I'd get rid of the chicken dinners. Too much work. Hamburgers are just as good, and quicker."

"And everyone likes hamburgers."

"That's right. If you're hungry, there's a little place about two blocks back that's fine."

"Thank you. Say, did you see that funny truck with the angel on it?"

"You mean Mother's boys? They was just in."

"What's that all about? Some kind of church?"

Carl frowned and scratched himself.

"Guess it depends on what you think church is. They're not my idea of Christians, but they're believers, anyway. Live up in the Santa Susanna canyon with a bunch of women, and folks say they all run around naked and worship this old gal called Mother. Course, folks say a lot of things. The fellows are always dressed proper and act nice enough when I seen 'em. Most of the women pick walnuts for Diamond, and they wouldn't stand for any nakedness there. What they do on their own time's their own business."

"So they're just harmless crackpots?"

"Just ordinary Californians, seems to me."

She thanked him and drove slowly through the little town, stopping at the place called Manny's which advertised "Ice Water." It was a white-washed, big-windowed box set back from the road, with a gravel parking lot rimmed with a ragged line of oaks. She sat at the counter and ate a bowl of bland chili with dry cornbread. She didn't talk to the waitress, and the waitress didn't talk to her.

She got a blanket out of the car and walked down the hill towards the little stream, forded it, and continued south. Soon she came to an orange orchard, set the blanket between the trees and lay down to rest. The late afternoon sunlight shone through the waxy leaves, and a steady drip-drip came from the irrigation lines. A mockingbird hopped close to her foot, snatched a loose piece of wool and flew away. Muriel shifted onto her left side and peered through the trunks towards the foothills. Somewhere out there, a cult lived by whatever odd rules its founders had set. It seemed very far away and not really her business.

It occurred to her that today was the nearest she'd ever been to a day trip away from work and the city with Ray, whom she adored. She was with him all day, and some nights, but never nights of her choosing. He was so often preoccupied, with his wife, with his friends, or with the bottle. Maybe this solitary experience was the best she was going to get, on the trail of a green panel truck that held the secrets needed to help her lover keep his job.

The thought annoyed her, and she batted it away.

Later, she walked back into town. A brilliant white motor court offered cottages by the night, and she booked herself one with a bath. The wall light was dim, and she squinted unpicking the hem of her blue dress, shedding a year of urban sophistication to better blend in with the hayseeds. It was still early as she slipped into sleep reading a true story magazine she'd found in the dresser, suspending disbelief to become enthralled in a convoluted narrative about a lovesick hairdresser with child.

Wherever Ray was now, she imagined he was thinking of her, or at least wondering where his car had gone. She was wrong.

Alice Dabney was a silly woman who had been forced into seriousness by circumstances. The new model did not suit her. She was dressed in man's pajamas, blue and white striped, rolled at the ankle. She refused out of vanity to bob her still-golden, wavy hair, and its mass lay coiled at the base of her neck like a small bird's breast. Her polished pink nails were bitten down to the quick. Slim fingers drummed nervously along her thigh.

She sat with Ray in the long sun porch at the back of the bungalow, with her small bottom perched at the edge of a deep Adirondack chair. Ray's chair had double-width arms, and she'd insisted on laying out a pot of tea, cup and saucer, and a plate of shortbread there. The arms sloped a bit, and made Ray nervous. Alice Dabney's odd mannerisms compounded the sense of unease.

She'd been eager to let him in, smiling in welcome even before he identified himself as Joseph Dabney's right-hand man. Her ease at her own undress was peculiar. The house was very dark and stale, and he had the sense in following her through it that she'd been sitting by the door waiting for him, for anyone, to knock and start talking.

It wasn't easy. She kept laughing at the wrong places and was slow to give polite, expected responses. He pushed on through the formalities, to the real reason for his call.

"—so you can understand why I am interested in knowing more about these women with whom your husband was in business."

"Are you very interested in business, Mr. Chandler?"

Her voice had a piping quality which might have been charming in a different woman. The question was, he thought, nonsensical, and he responded in kind.

"I am as interested in business as a businessman should be, Mrs. Dabney. How about you?"

"Oh, I suppose I'm interested in all kinds of things. But tell me, are you married?"

"I am."

"And do you think of your marriage as a business arrangement, Mr. Chandler?"

She was perhaps, he mused, not as silly as she seemed.

"No, Mrs. Dabney, I do not."

"Well, when you say 'these women with whom my husband was in business,' I must say you mis-categorize, quite as much as if you said 'my wife, with whom I am in business.' Mrs. Blackburn and Mrs. Rizzio are our souls' mates, and I truly do not know why my husband would have sent someone like you to ask questions about our private, family affairs. No offense to you, Mr. Chandler. You seem like a gentleman. But I trust you understand my feelings on the matter."

She stamped her slippered feet and waited. He sighed, and gave her his most charming smile. In spite of her pique, she returned it. He charmed ahead.

"Oh, my dear lady. I know this is must be an imposition. Can you possibly forgive me? It's only at the direction of my employer, Mr. Dabney senior, that I've come at all. I have no wish to embarrass or distress you in any way. Maybe you can help me to understand, and I won't have to bother you any more. This pamphlet, for instance."

He pulled from his pocket the top book in the stack, the one Ward had called the first revelation. Alice Dabney made a noise, darted forward, and snatched it from his fingers. She raised the front of the pamphlet to her lips and kissed the face of the angel, then clutched the paper tight to her chest, angel side down.

"May I keep it, Mr. Chandler? My husband has taken all the revelations away."

He looked away, shamed by her ardor, and muttered, "Of course, it's yours."

She was suddenly uncertain. "Oh, but one is supposed to share the revelations. I shouldn't take it from you."

"Please, Mrs. Dabney. I insist. I can get another. But why don't you tell me about the revelation? That's a form of sharing, too. Tell me. And I'll go then, I promise."

She turned the pamphlet in her hands, and made a soft, happy sound. Then she smiled, closed her eyes and spoke.

"I suppose there's no harm in it, not really. Oh, how can I tell you? I imagine it will sound strange. Well, I suppose I should begin with once upon a time."

"Please do. What was it that happened, once upon a time?"

"It was that there were two earthly women who discovered that they could hear the voice of the angel Gabriel. The voice called them to a city named for the angels, and helped them to gather a community of friends. Each night, the earthly women transcribed holy words of the angel Gabriel, and each day they schooled their friends in the wisdom of the stars. Every one of the friends was given a Concord, by which to demonstrate their dedication to the cause."

"Did you count things, Mrs. Dabney?"

She tittered. "No, counting is for our simple friends. It is good for their minds. My Concord involved maintaining a physical posture, and because of this I was known as The Holy Keystone, the upholding arch between heaven and earth. Each member of the community contributed in the way to which they were suited, and together we were completing the Great Work. It's most fulfilling."

"But I thought that both you and your husband wished to leave the group—that you wanted your money back because the book wasn't finished?"

"Certainly not! Mr. Chandler, I'm sure I don't have to tell you how the Dabneys are. My husband, like his uncle, is a greedy man. No worldly acquisition is ever quite enough for him. But we learned that the Great Work does not keep to human timetables. Our household contributed everything we were meant to, with our money, yes, and with our Concords. The Great Work was not yet completed, but it was further along, and others were coming into the community to give of themselves and their assets. But of course, that wasn't good enough for Clifford. He pretended to understand the revelations, but what he really wanted was to be important. He wanted it to be his money that finished the Great Work, and when that didn't happen, he turned on Mother and on Ruth, and on all our friends. He ran crying to his uncle. He sent you here!"

She shook her head. "No, Mr. Chandler. I do not want my money back. I want my friends back. I want to be there when the Great Work is completed, not shut up in this house like a punished child."

"Why don't you go back to your friends, then? Don't they meet just over on Manhattan Place?"

She laughed again, but there was no humor in it. "I can't go anywhere. Clifford locked all my clothes in the closet, and he didn't leave me any money." She ran her hands over the pajamas in disgust. "When you see your employer, will you ask him to send some shoes and dresses to his nephew's wife?"

Shamed again, he turned away and said he certainly would. He finished his tea, because she insisted, and he left her house. It was only on the streetcar, a few blocks from his office, that he realized he had forgotten to ask where Clifford Dabney was staying.

Tom was already settled in a booth on the Family Entrance side when Ray arrived at Good Fellows Grotto, that venerable oyster house beloved by the City Hall crowd. George led him back through the little coves of curtained booths, some emitting the sounds of illicit communion, others the hearty tones of back room politics as usual.

The dusty chandeliers tinkled in the ceiling fan breeze, and on autographed posters the luscious bodies of opera stars and vaudeville queens seemed to quiver, too. Wood smoke wafted out from the kitchen, and blended with the fumes from fine cigars. The room surged with unrepressed voices, a mingled stew of Italian, French, English, Yiddish, with the infrequent tinkling of feminine laughter tying them all together in the unmistakable language of the place.

A visit to the Grotto was a trip back to the Los Angeles Ray had known as a young man fresh from Europe, agape at the raw possibility of this new continent and city on the make. There were no Iowa puritans within these walls, just people who took life in their fists and made something out of it. He had here on his birthday gorged himself on sweetbreads, laughed so hard he'd had to hold onto his chair to

52

keep from toppling over, woken up once in the corner of the kitchen with no memory of how he'd come to be there. He'd wooed his still-married wife behind drawn curtains. The Grotto was more than a restaurant—it was a friend.

Tom had changed into a perfectly presentable suit, and looked like a traffic cop masquerading as an undertaker. Ray sometimes thought it was Tom's hangdog features that had doomed him to fail in the seat of power, even more than his insufferable decency.

But still, he said, and mostly meant, "You clean up nicely, Mr. James."

"It's not often I have a dinner date. Why not make an occasion of it? So, tell me. How do you like the detective trade?"

"Oh, it's wonderful. Half the city saw me conversing with a mustachioed lunatic in a lady's bathrobe, I took my tea with a woman dressed in her husband's pajamas—oh, and my secretary stole my car. Remind me to do more detecting. It's enormously amusing. I did get these, though." Ray pulled from his briefcase some files from Dabney's desk and a full set of the revelatory pamphlets.

He called for wine, and told Tom about the day's discoveries over bouillabaisse into which they dipped thick crusts of toast. They speculated about what course their investigation would take next, with Ray taking a scientific interest in the tools available to Tom, legal and otherwise. The steaks were thick and perfect, the crab cold and fresh as the North Sea, and Ray taught Tom how to eat his peas properly, with a knife.

Their business largely settled, Tom asked after Ray's wife, as was proper. But Ray just waved his hands in front of his face and screwed his mouth up, like he'd bitten into a lemon. "She's not a happy woman," was all he said. There being no proper response to that information, Tom said only, "I am so sorry."

Over the course of the meal, Ray had drunk most of two carafes of the house Dago Red, and by the time the diplomat puddings were served, he was feeling sorry for himself. And although he and Tom were not intimate friends, the good food and the convivial atmosphere made it easy to speak intimately. And, too, it seemed that his mind was looping in angry circles, and he couldn't have stopped his tongue without an effort that was beyond him.

"Muriel's a lovely girl, isn't she? Smart, spunky, very fond of me. Deserves all the good things in life. And what do I do? Slink off to my wife, leave her sitting up alone in a hotel suite only suited for a whore's bed. She had every right to steal my car—if she did steal it. Why am I sitting here stuffing myself, when that lovely girl might be in danger? What's wrong with me, Tom? Why can't I love anyone?"

He pushed the footed bowl away and put his head on the table, grinding his cheekbone into the cloth as if he wanted to erase himself.

Tom slipped around to Ray's side of the table, and lifted him gently upright.

"Hush now. That's not true. You know it isn't. You're just having a bad night."

"I'm having a bad life! I've done everything the wrong way round. I hurt everybody. It's only right I should suffer, too."

"Now Ray—Ray my boy, there there—stop that. Come on, we'll go. Come home with me. You can't go back to your wife in this condition. I'm sure Muriel will call in the morning, and we'll know everything is fine. She's a brave girl, resourceful. Waiter! Check please!"

Ray sat up and clawed at his inside pocket, stumbling over his billfold and spilling cash out over the table. "It's to be my treat. You're my friend and I'm buying you dinner. Mateo! Mateo, come here right now!"

But Mateo Dujmovitch was already standing alongside the table, and together he and Tom peeled the drunken man from the booth, helped him down the sidewalk and into the back of Tom's car. Once off his feet, Ray started snoring. Under wool blankets on Tom's davenport he slept fitfully through dawn.

Four

Tom lived in a suite of rooms on the second floor of his foster mother's spacious bungalow. When Allie Wheeler's daughter was still unmarried (and before her husband's passing) he'd been comfortable enough in the finished loft above the garage, but changes in the family had changed his role, as well.

Allie was old enough to be his grandmother, and she was probably his best friend on earth. He couldn't count the nights they'd sat up, debating the state of the world and strategizing ways of improving life for those who would accept a little help. It was Allie who'd supported him when the call of police work eclipsed the ministry, who'd bought the books and journals that lined his study walls—sociology, political science, criminology, philosophy—and who had booked the train ticket that took him from Beaver Dam, Kentucky, to Los Angeles, her home, a city he had come to adore even as it tore his heart out.

Together, they'd canvassed the city's churches, assuring fellow Christians and temperance workers that a vote for John C. Porter would shine a much needed beacon into the dark and worldly crevices of City Hall. Porter had welcomed their enthusiasm, and said all the right things to buoy the spirits of the spiritual. It was only after the election, when he set his rump upon the big man's chair, that the devil's smile showed through.

And Tom had been sitting right beside the Mayor, privileged to be the great man's personal Police Commission investigator, when the obviously altered civil service list came across the desk showing how Vice Squad man Roy Steckel was positioned to move up in the world. Nothing Tom said about Steckel's reputation within the force as a brute and an opportunist seemed to make the slightest impression on Porter, who merely smiled and reminded Tom that they were all big boys with a big a city to run, and that he shouldn't make an ass of himself.

Allie had held his head while he sobbed, ironed the rumples from his brown suit, handed him her own handkerchief and sent him back to work, reminding him that God worked in strange ways. Porter wasn't stupid; he was slick as an eel. They'd never known he was a Klansman, that he drank, that he loved money just like the rest of the dirty ones. Having helped preach the man into office, Tom had made it his business to preach him out again. Soon enough, he was cut from the investigator's rolls and dumped on the traffic beat, at 7th and Broadway, the center of the universe.

He was shamed, but Allie saw the glory in the position. So many ears to which to minister! All of those people crossing his intersection, on their way to the banks of Spring Street—the grand department stores—the restaurants—the theater—even scientists catching the streetcar to Caltech. Citizens all. And so he did his job, one which she had helped him see was much bigger than his $200 monthly salary, his bunions and his sunburn. She helped him not to despair of his circumstances, but to see each challenge as merely one more rung in a climb towards a better world.

And this was his life in late summer, 1929.

Ray settled himself under the folds of the red Hudson Bay blanket, bare white feet sticking out the end. Tom looked up through the open door of his study. The morning was cool, with fog still soft on the hills.

It had been a rough night. Ray was quiet enough coming up the stairs, but once he was laid flat he demanded that Tom hold his hand and talk with him, or else, he threatened, he wouldn't be responsible for his actions. Tom did as he was asked, listening between regular hushed reminders to keep it down, not to wake the house. And so in a whisper, Ray spoke bitterly about his wife, his failed literary ambi-

58

tions, about his dead mother, his loneliness, his frustrations at work.

Finally, in the middle of a confusing complaint about legal maneuverings surrounding an oil strike, he slept, and Tom pulled his numb hand free and fell into his own bed a room away.

It was nearly 9 on Saturday, and the house was coming to life. With each soft knock downstairs, Ray stirred and grumbled, and soon the mix of women's voices and clattering china shook him into semi-consciousness. Taking stock of his surroundings with the measured gaze of a man who not infrequently woke in strange places, he nodded at Tom, ran fingers through his hair, shook his head several times, hooked a thumb in one belt loop, then dashed down the hall to the toilet, where he vomited. When he came out again, he was pale, but composed. Together they walked down the steps into a parlor filled with older ladies of all sorts. Allie's friends from the Women's Christian Temperance Union were in residence.

The appearance of young men stirred the women into a blaze of action. Allie ushered them into the twin Morris chairs that flanked the fireplace, Hester brought coffee and powdered sugar donuts on a silver tray, and Della, sitting on the piano stool, swung around and knocked out a bit of ragtime because she knew Tom liked it. Tom introduced Ray

59

simply as his British friend in the oil business, but it wasn't long before Allie had pried the whole story out of them, and sent Tom back upstairs for the mystical pamphlets.

For half an hour, the long room was a seminar, with the ladies reading to themselves and occasionally interjecting observations, passing the books back and forth and cross-referencing phrases in the Bible and concordance. There was laughter and tut-tutting, and anecdotes about odd religious services attended, or heard about.

"That man Knox who says he found Hell with his telescope—"

"In Glendale—so funny! 'How long will Hell burn?'"

"And of course Mrs. McPherson's theatricals—"

"Only in Hollywood. I rather liked that theater on Grand, though, what are they called, the Theosophicals?"

"Theosophists. I heard they have Russian roots."

"Oh, that explains the tea. I hate strong tea."

"More coffee, Hester?"

"Why, yes, please."

More chatter, more reading. Then Allie, who had gone methodically through each booklet in order, called Tom and Ray over to the library table and gave them the benefit of her interpretation.

"These females are mad! Oh, not entirely. There is some internal logic in their writing, and a reasonable familiarity with the Old Testament and Mrs. Baker Eddy. But these little books were written without any editing, and maybe without even looking back to see what had gone into the one before. And such silly little language games! Olive trees and O LIVE and Abraham Lincoln and the sin of Ham—pure drivel. If your Mr. Dabney fell for what they had to offer, it wasn't because he read these books."

Ray smiled. "I'm not entirely sure my Mr. Dabney knows how to read."

"Oh, but it does sound as if this Mrs. Blackburn could preach," said Della. "And a really good preacher can get inside your bones, even if all they're selling is personality and snake oil."

"And the daughter is rather voluptuous," noted Tom.

"Well, there you go, then," said Allie. "Of course, one can't say just by looking at a chapbook if this sect has any real faith in it, or if it's simply a matter of economics. It is rather different if they believe this stuff themselves, you know. You'd be astonished how much it can cost to run a bare-bones church in this city. It's entirely possible that they took everything Mr. Dabney had, and simply spent it on the needs of the organization—no larceny in it at all."

"It doesn't matter to me if they believe it," said Ray. "I just have to find out where the money went. If they built a fine little chapel with it, very well, and I'll report that. And if they spent it on ruby-studded Ouija boards, it's all the same to me. Dabney either doesn't know or doesn't want to say. But somebody knows."

"And I'm quite sure you'll find out, with my Tom helping you," purred Allie, with a loving look.

"They might be quite wicked," piped Della, who was unsuitably thrilled at the idea. "They might even be dangerous!"

"We'll be careful. But whatever they are, Ray and I aim to find out. We're planning to attend one of their teaching sessions. I'm curious to hear what they sound like when they're preaching to the believers, and to well-situated newcomers they hope to welcome into the fold."

Ray went about the room gathering up the pamphlets, now splayed out and some with bits of sugar clinging to their pages.

Allie cleared the breakfast things away with Tom's help. Then turning at the kitchen door, she spoke softly to her foster son. "I know I don't have to remind you not to be seduced by graven idols."

"I'll be careful, ma'am."

Tom eased his car out onto the slim wedge of Reno Street, the last, short diagonal block before the American surveyors had bent the old Spanish city to a strict east/west orientation. After her husband's death and her inheritance of the Wheeler Tract, Allie had had her choice of sites for a homestead. She'd selected this odd corner of the city because it amused her to be situated between the old and new world, and because it was unpretentious. The better plots had been sold or developed, the income used for her support, political campaigns and her family's education.

They were both quiet on the drive. Ray rested his head against the hot window and fought back a wave of nausea. Tom thought how strange it was that he'd felt so comfortable bringing a drunken man into a prohibitionist home, and that he'd scarcely considered that the ladies might think ill of Ray, though unshaven and reeking of wine-sweat.

Ray was, he believed, a victim of his thirst. He drank because he was sad, and the sadness fed on the drink and grew stronger. Sober, he was kind and intelligent enough that the occasional excesses were tolerable—for now. A belief in temperance didn't preclude associating with someone who failed to practice this ideal, but he did hope that Ray would come to see the light. Until that time, Tom's choice was to say nothing about it, and to be his friend.

They parted on the sidewalk with plans to meet again on Sunday, when they would attend the spiritualist gathering on Manhattan Place.

Tom could hear Ray's apologetic tones even before he opened the door of his upstairs flat. From within, a woman's voice rose in a shrill indictment, and something heavy was thrown against a wall. Ray ducked inside, and Tom turned away, grateful for his simple life. Then, tired of thinking, he went to an alley, cold and loud, and bowled into the afternoon.

Five

It wasn't perfect, or even pleasant, but it was home and Ray had gotten used to it. Cissy's emotional palate, which had been mercurial early in their relationship, had settled into simmering irritation, which flashed into momentary rage whenever he did something that annoyed her. It annoyed her when he made too much noise in the bath, when he got a snag in the fabric of his trousers, when he forgot the eggs, or when he remembered them but put them on the second shelf instead of the first. She didn't like music in the house any more, so he didn't put any on.

It was easier, he'd found, to keep his head down and appease her than to try to argue. And she found it easiest of all to lash out and storm off, to lick her imagined and sometimes real wounds in silent solitude.

Today, she couldn't even be bothered to yell at him for long. She made a few choice remarks and went into her bedroom, claiming a headache. She didn't need to tell Ray not to follow. There was nothing he wanted to do less.

On his desk, he found a small pile of notes, neat at the bottom, less so at the top, alerting him to a series of calls from Muriel. No number. The only message was that she would call again.

He showered and shaved, quietly, combed tonic through his hair, then took the documents from Dabney's desk out onto the balcony to read. When the phone rang, he ran for it, but Cissy had beat him to the cradle. She gave him a smile that would frost a glass and trilled, "It's your secretary, darling."

He wrestled the receiver from her hand and turned his back. Cissy shoved him half-heartedly and stomped off.

"Muriel, are you all right? Where are you?"

Her voice sounded small and lively down the wire. "I'm fine! Followed the truck practically to Ventura County. Found out quite a bit already. I know where they're living, and I've got an idea how I can make friends with them."

"You're not coming back?"

"Not right away. Want to follow a couple of threads first. I've got a job, sorting walnuts, of all things! That's what the lady faithful do, and I'm going to see what I can learn from being friendly. Maybe they'll invite me home for supper."

"Don't be foolish. These people could be dangerous. I think you should come back, let Tom handle the undercover work—or me."

"Don't you be foolish, Ray. Tom looks like a cop, you look like an oil company executive. You sound like one, too. I'm the only one out of us who can blend in with normal people, and I'm doing just fine. And anyway, I think it's rather nice—getting out of the city, I mean. Did you know it was sweet-corn season? I didn't. I'll be back a day or two. You can live without your car that long."

"I don't care about the car. I care about you."

"Well, thanks. I'm glad you answered the phone. I don't think your wife could have taken another message." There was a pause, and static filled the line.

"Are you still there, Pipsy?"

"Where were you last night?"

"With Tom. We read the little books that I got from Weird Ward, and I stayed with him. Tom's foster mother is quite religious. Anyway, she knows a lot about religion. She thinks the writing is balderdash, just a mess of the Bible and Christian Science, but that it's possible that May and Ruth believe all this stuff."

"Hmm. Well, I'll see what I can find out about that."

"But how can I reach you?"

"No phone. I'll call you. Don't worry. Be good!"

There was plenty of work in the nut factory, the manager had told Muriel. "You can have one shift, or more if you want it. Come in any time you want to pick up some wages. Most of the girls like the evening shift. It's cooler. We pay by the hour, with a bonus if you're quick."

Standing at the dusty mirror in the empty locker room, she fastened the white smock dress around her waist and pinned the white cap into her hair. From the factory came the aircraft whirr of industrial fans and belts, and a low murmur of conversation. It was hot, and the angled bands of sunlight through the room-wide windows were nearly solid with whirling motes. She tied a kerchief around her neck and stepped into the big room where double rows of sweaty, white-clad ladies were busily snatching at the nuts rolling past them.

The older woman who'd given her the uniform and locker key led Muriel to an open spot in the U-shaped line and showed her how to sort the whole nuts into seven grades, as distinguished in the labeled boxes stacked on racks behind her stool, and where to toss the broken bits. When a box was full, she was to place it by her feet, and a boy would retrieve and weigh it, and credit her account. Muriel looked sadly at her doomed manicure, cracked her knuckles, and began.

The work was mindless, and the experienced workers talked among themselves while sorting. Muriel soon found she had the hang of the simple job, and began to listen in. Nearest to her, on her right and across, were a pair of pretty dark women, apparently sisters, who joked softly in Spanish. Down at the end of the U, under the big fan, she noticed a group of eight white women, all middle aged, who seemed to move together with the nervous sympathies of a clutch of hens. These were, she thought, the most likely prospects to be members of the cult. She hoped they were friendly to outsiders.

The dinner break was her chance to find out. The women had a wicker basket, and two of them were methodically unpacking it at a picnic table under an old oak while the others waited quietly. Muriel had a sandwich in her locker, but played it dumb. "Say, could I buy a little dinner from you ladies tonight? It's my first shift, and I didn't think to bring anything to eat."

The ladies looked at one another over their basket and seemed to reach some wordless conclusion. The taller of the pair turned to her and said, "Of course, you'll sit down and eat with us as our guest. We've plenty, don't we, sisters?" There were nods and murmurs of assent, and Muriel stepped forward to take her place at the table.

Six

Ray skimmed the slim pile of papers from Dabney's office, but found nothing of consequence, just bills from the tailor, receipts from past travels, a few rough drawings of some sort of tractor with an elevated seat. Around four, Cissy rapped on the door jamb, came in and laid a covered dish on his desk. She stood there looking at him until he made a comedy flourish and lifted the lid. Under it were six triangles of thin toast, spread to their edges with a dark brown jelly. The smell of fish wafted out and Ray grinned foolishly.

"Oh, Cissikins, where ever did you find it?"

"I asked Mr. Oviatt to bring a tub back for you."

Ray had formed an abiding affection for Gentleman's Relish, Patum Peperium, at his uncle's table in England, but there was no market for the fragrant stuff in America and he'd long since stopped offering to share his occasional findings.

"That was quite sweet of you," he mused.

"Tuck in. It's best when it's hot, isn't it?"

"Mmmm." He ate the snack, and she sat nearby as if she didn't find him completely repulsive, and when he had finished she didn't move to leave. The relish had been a surprise to him, but not her changed aspect. They were expected at Alma Lloyd's for dinner, and neither wanted to spoil that pleasure. Alma was among their oldest Los Angeles friends, and it was to her lively, loving home that they were ever drawn on holidays and in times of need.

It was in the library of the old house, the mansion on Bonnie Brae, that Cissy and Ray had met. This was before Warren had died, when the Lloyd children were still small. Ray was newly returned from the service and had slipped easily back into his role as something of an Old World pet the Lloyds had picked up on the transatlantic crossing, and in whose career and literary pretensions they took an interest.

Cissy and her husband Julian were typical of the Lloyds' artistic friends. He was musical, she elegant and witty. In dusty Los Angeles, so provincial and small, it was natural that a group of intelligent folk would make their own fun in private spaces. It was as an inside joke against themselves that Warren named their club of moody souls The Optimists—yet strangely, they had felt happier once they took the name.

It was in this charmed space that Ray had realized he desired Julian's titian-haired wife, had confided in Alma, had begun the cold process of carving a man's mate away through a communal assault of logic, passion and intrigue. Now he had her, and he loved her—he supposed. But sometimes he thought back on those days and wondered if he hadn't been a little insane, and if the whole love affair might not have died out in a season if not for the flame fanned by their whole social circle, so invested in its consummation.

He felt unsettled when he found himself questioning the myth of their great love affair. Wasn't Cissy still beautiful and bright? Didn't she treat him more tenderly than not, when her mood was fine? And anyway, if he didn't want her, who would? She was his responsibility now, and perhaps always.

Warren was gone and the children were grown, and Alma lived alone in more modest circumstances, occupying a roomy garden apartment somewhat cramped with favorite things. But the aging remnants of The Optimists still gathered faithfully, several times each month, to play cards, discuss books, and keep their human ties alive. They owed that much to Warren's memory, and their own remembered selves.

And so it was that Ray and Cissy stood at Alma's door, his arm grazing her subtle velvet waist. She tucked her head against his shoulder and they were framed there, perfect lovers, as the door opened, revealing the faces of friends. Estelle, Alma's daughter, ushered them inside. She was just returned from Europe, with much to tell Cissy. They disappeared down the hall to the little room where the ladies left their wraps and bags, and did whatever it was ladies did out of sight of men.

Ray meanwhile made his way to the bar and poured a highball, not too strong. He greeted his hostess and complimented her until she was called into the kitchen. Then he followed Manly Hall's piping voice to the library, where he found as expected a small group of women gathered around the mystic, their eager forms reflected in the dark silk cape skimming his big shoulders.

If he were a greedy man, Chandler might detest Manly Hall. Like Chandler, Hall's life had been much changed by friendship with the Lloyds. But instead of being set on the tracks of a career, the charismatic Canadian had benefited through classic patronage. His astonishing metaphysical library, funded by the family, his esoteric publications, his world travels, the proposed institute near Griffith Park, all of it hastened by Estelle's generosity. The total cost of her kindness, he'd heard whispered, approached a million dollars.

But he'd passed up his own opportunity to play house with young Estelle, and there were no hard feelings. And she was justly proud of her role in helping to make her beneficiary an intellectual force to reckon with. There was nobody else who better understood the astonishing blend of

East and West that was happening in this city on the edge of the Pacific shore, or who could sort the manifestly inspired from the phonies who used faith to prey on the weak. If the Blackburn gang were sincere, Hall would know it.

At the center of the charmed circle, he held a small volume open to an illustrated page. Despite his pointing finger, all eyes were on his face.

"But the marvelous thing is that without even knowing how to read, without having any advanced education, or libraries, or written history to draw upon, these tribesmen can remember and speak about generations of experience. One cannot underestimate the ability of the human mind to record its own actions."

"Hall, have you a moment?"

"Chandler, hello. Certainly." He excused himself from his audience, and the men stepped out onto the patio.

"I've got a spiritual problem—" Ray began.

"I must confess, I'm surprised to hear that from you! But happy to advise, of course."

Ray laughed. "It's something that's come up in the office. Joseph Dabney has a nephew, silly kid—a playboy. He's gotten himself involved with a religious group called The Great Eleven, or possibly The Branch. I've been asked to provide a report on this organization, and to track their financial dealings with young Dabney. I wondered if you've run across them in your travels."

Hall nodded, and when he spoke now it was without his performer's expansiveness, but with an actuarial precision.

"The Great Eleven. A mother and daughter act, with a robed masculine emissary who sells booklets on the street. Low-profile outfit—they don't advertise—but they've been in town quite a while. I've met a few of the more casual followers, at my lectures, though never the initiates or leaders. There was a young man who came to see me recently, with some notion of training his mind to be more pure so that he'd be a suitable marriage partner for the daughter. I suggested he purchase a copy of my monograph, but he said he'd been forbidden to read modern books."

"Arthur Osborne. Do you find that strange?"

"Oh, it's common enough in these little sects. They seek to control the information that their followers obtain—to simplify the message and make it easier for differing personalities to commune. I don't think it's necessarily sinister—though of course it wouldn't suit an intelligent seeker. That said, not all seekers are intelligent, and who are we to judge the emotional hungers of those less gifted than ourselves?"

"Well, Dabney's out $40,000 in money they've spent printing these flimsy pamphlets and I don't know what else. And now that he's broke, the big shots don't take his calls. I've been around long enough to spot the back end of a long con."

"Hmm. Maybe. But there might be less to it. Many times, a weak person will use their financial assets to increase their importance in a group. This is common in all societies. When the money stops moving around, the roles change. That's natural, and while unpleasant, I suspect that this is not a new experience for your Mr. Dabney."

"Indeed. Have you heard about any holdings of this group? Property, in town or elsewhere?"

"No. I've got no idea where they stay. What does Dabney say?"

"Not much. Not yet. There's a house on Manhattan where they give classes, but I think it's rented. I'll keep digging. I've got to have a story to tell the old man, something he can understand. I don't think he'll be satisfied with the idea that his nephew gave a fortune away for printer's ink. There's got to be an angle. Everyone has got an angle."

"Perhaps, but don't be so sure that the members of this sect aren't sincere. In my experience, it's just as likely that they're true believers as that they worship more material things. Keep asking questions. I like to see you with your teeth sunk into a mystery. But be careful—the ideas you stir up may prove disruptive to your psychic comfort."

"I guess I can handle a little mental disruption. It's the babysitting of millionaires that wears me out."

"Ever our burden, dear Chandler. Come, let's go back to the ladies and enjoy the night."

Hall resumed his informal lecture in the library, and after a few moments, Ray slipped away. He made another drink, this one not so pale. Conversations caught and lost him, and he moved through the rooms with no particular direction. He kept missing Cissy, or she him, but it didn't bother him. Then dinner was served, and he was proud to sit opposite her, with her queen-like manner and creamy skin picking up glints from the peridot sparklers in her ears. The food and conversation were fine, just fine. There was nothing to find fault with, yet something nagged at his thoughts.

Then later, in the kitchen, he was trying to teach Eddie Lloyd and his wife how to make a proper hot punch, and he cut his finger when preparing the lemon rind and the juice stung smartly. He spilled sugar down his vest and gummed up his pocket watch. The room felt hot, she laughed at him, and he stomped out.

Back at the party, he looked for Cissy, but she wasn't in sight. He thought he caught Julian Pascal giving him a pitying look, and briefly considered knocking him off his piano stool. But instead he went out into the garden, then around the side of the building, where he stood for a long time, his elbow on the ashcan, looking up at the diffused, starless light of the sky. He realized it was Muriel that was bothering him, and wondered if he was falling in love with her. That was idiotic. He breathed the night air a while longer, and went back inside.

He resumed his circuit of conversations, like a fish in a bowl. He kept missing Cissy, and wondered if she planned it that way. They ran out of the Canadian whiskey and hating the Mexican sort, he changed over to gin. God, it was bright in here. He sat down. Alma asked him if he was all right. Of course he was all right. Then Cissy was there, and she looked annoyed. He felt her hands on his waist and went to embrace her, but she was only fishing for the car keys.

"Don't make a scene," she hissed. As if he ever made a scene. It really was hot, though. Then they were out on the sidewalk and he was sucking on his sore finger and tasting sugar. He couldn't be bothered to snatch the keys back, or even to make fun of her driving. They started home. She said something mean, and he returned the favor.

He wasn't even angry, but she was. Looking ahead, spine erect, lips tight around her teeth, she purred that if he didn't like the way things were, it would be quite all right with her if he went away to stay.

"You keep the car, I'll keep the furniture, and we can forget we ever played this whole charade, hmm? But I think you'll find it harder to forget me, dear husband. You're just like your father. You lush."

Suddenly angry, too, he grunted something and flopped over on his side, and though she shoved him, and hard, he played dead.

He must have fallen asleep, because the next thing he knew it was morning, and he was baking inside the closed up car half a block from their flat. She'd picked a spot with no shade at all, and tossed a blanket over him before going up to bed. To spite her, he blew his nose into his palm and rubbed the muck off on the passenger side upholstery. If it was war she wanted, she could have it.

Seven

They stood side by side by the great mirrored wall of the Athletic Club men's room, with its cool green fixtures that made them feel like they were under the sea. Ray was fussing.

"Now, Tom, lift your collar, like so. And bring a little bit of hair down onto your brow. That's perfect—look at you!"

"Yes, look at me. I look like a prize nincompoop."

"You look like a prize fish, mouth wide for the hook. We'll catch more flies with money than with vinegar, and the Great Eleven is going to just love you as a wayward millionaire on a quest for enlightenment."

"Do I have to talk like a longhair?"

"Talk like yourself. You don't have to do anything other than imagine you've got a nice juicy oil lease or two in your back pocket that you might be willing to sign over if the right 'growth opportunity' came along. Here, put these in your wallet, for inspiration." Ray took a pile of crisp bank-notes from his billfold, snapped them into a bright money clip, and slid the lot across the shelf.

"Don't let me forget to give this back to you."

"Oh, honestly, Tom. It's from petty cash. Dabney can afford it. Take Allie out to a show. Now, odds are you won't even have to talk about money, except to pay for the lesson with a large bill. You're wearing enough gold to make an impression. We'll give them a little taste of you, and see if you're tasty enough to bring the big rats out of their hole. And in the meantime, maybe we'll learn something. If nothing else, Ward Blackburn is a giggle."

"Come on, let's go. My forehead itches."

Manhattan Place was a block of solid two-story homes that had been moderately fashionable in the middle 'teens. Soon after, big brick apartment houses had filled in the empty lots, and now the street felt more than a little shabby. Those with means had decamped for points west, while the suckers held on and dreamed of better days.

Number 640 was a broad-porched Chinese bungalow coated in a clot of dull green shingles. A river rock chimney scratched the sky. The narrow driveway was stacked with cars straight back to the property line, none of them new. Tom pulled around the block and parked out of sight on Sixth Street. It wouldn't suit a millionaire to be seen emerging from a four-year-old Buick sedan.

The front door was unlatched and a hand-lettered placard in the lace-curtained window read SUNDAY SERVICE – ALL WELCOME. Ray gave a brisk shave-and-a-haircut knock, one hand on the knob to keep the door from flying open. From within, a woman's voice sang "Come on i-i-i-nnnn!"

The entry hall was papered in pale speckled green, with brown velvet curtains framing the doors to either side. A wide wooden stair wound up and to the left, with the requisite fern on the landing. An owlish young woman appeared at the left doorway and made a hurried welcoming gesture. They followed. In the parlor, two dozen disparate souls sat on white-washed folding chairs, facing east.

At the end of the room, behind a lectern, a tall, slender man with swooping dark mustaches under a long aquiline nose was in the midst of a dramatic recitation. To his left, a sad-eyed, heavyset woman crouched to scribble his words onto a small blackboard set on an easel. On the wall behind them hung linen panels embroidered with mirror images of the group's angelic emblem. Double rows of musical notes poured from the two trumpets. At the center, the music met, twined together and exploded into a blue and silver star.

Tom and Ray took their places in the back.

"Moon Stone. Moon's Tone," said the man, drawing the vowel sounds out to the length of his exhalations.

"Ahhhhhhhh!" said the worshippers as one, as they rose, hands aloft and palms forward. Ray and Tom stood politely.

"Olive. O live." These phrases were sung, in the dramatic Jewish fashion.

"Eeeeeeeeeeee!" exclaimed the body, their wrists bent now like broken branches.

"Sit thee down! Yes, you too, Martha."

The people clattered into their seats, old joints cracking on man and on chair. The sad-eyed woman set her chalk behind her ear and took the open place beside Ray.

"Now of the moonstone," cried the man, "This is what the book says! Will you listen?"

He looked out over the room, with warm eyes that glowed with curiosity. When he came to the newcomers, he added a small nod of welcome. When each person had been individually acknowledged, he asked again, "Will you listen?"

The worshippers cupped their ears, leaned forward, and placed their hands upon their knees.

"Then listen, O! And God said to May and Ruth, 'Go down to the beach at Santa Monica, California. God has something there for you to do.'

"And God commanded them to walk along the shore close to the water, and God said to May, 'Pick up that moonstone quickly, before the waves sweep it out. It is a special moonstone that God has prepared for the work in the Sixth

Seal.' And God said, 'Take the moonstone home and God will command you what to do.'

"And May and Ruth obeyed diligently every command. And God said, 'Moonstone is double and it has two meanings; for it is the moon stone, and it is the moon's tone. The moon stone represents the minerals invisible in the water of God, and the moon's tone represents the seven tones of the word visible on the land of God.'

"And God said, 'The moonstone is the mother stone of all minerals and the foundation of all jewels and precious mines of the stars of heaven and earth. In the moonstone, I have placed the five great minerals.'

"Yes! Silica! Alumina! Potash! Soda! And the Lime! Just as the rainbow is all colors, and no color, the moonstone is all gems in a single body. And the five minerals do coincide to the five fingers of the hand, and to the five senses, too.

"God said this to May and Ruth, and this was true."

"Iiiiiiiiiiiiiiiiiiiiii," cried the faithful, with rattling chests. The weird sound set Ray's teeth on edge.

"Very good! Yes! Now as to the olive. Is it not so that the Lamb's Book of Life contains the two olive trees because olive means O LIVE? The Lamb's Book of Life would have to be at one with the quality O LIVE in order to be the Book of Life, so that the whole world of God's good people can read The Lamb's Book of Life—and can live."

"Ooooooooooo, it is soooooooo!" the body breathed, flapping their arms like chicken wings.

"Yes, but if you look on it on the wrong side, it is not the good olive tree, but the wicked EVIL O—evil naught, or nothing—which means that the evil is also nothing. If you do believe."

"We believe!" the worshippers exclaimed. They clamped their arms around themselves and executed a little chair-bound shimmy.

"Yes! And is it not so that there are six months in the year, and six seals, and six thousand years have passed since Adam? It takes 6000 years for a complete circuit to be made at the top of our solar system, all the while our watches are going at the rate of sixty seconds to make a minute here on earth.

"The Father is the five senses and the Mother is the seven tones. Five! And seven! The six houses that curse is the breathing out of the five senses of the Father—EVIL O. The six houses that bless is the breathing in of the seven tones of the Mother—O LIVE. And so we live between two poles— EVIL O! O LIVE!"

"EVIL O! O LIVE! EVIL O! O LIVE!"

"That's right. Very well." He shut the thin volume before him and stepped away from the lectern. "Next time, we will speak of the osculation of Dan and Naphtali, the head and the knees. And we will speak of the neck of God and all manner of thing that pass through it. So it is written. But I see we have newcomers among us today. Welcome, friends."

The faithful stood as a body, turned to face the strangers and bowed as deep as mainly aged spines allowed. Seen head on, they were a motley assortment, kind of face, unfashionably attired, none of them the sort of person one would notice if you passed them on the street. The Iowa type. Only Ward Blackburn, with his Chinese mustaches and claws, now in ordinary clothing, stood out as typical of a California sectarian.

Ward made a little hopping motion and ran up to Ray, grasped his arm and exclaimed, "You came! I knew you would come!"

"Well you made it sound so interesting, Ward. I thought I'd drop in and find out what the Sixth Seal is all about." He shook Ward off, but kindly, then turned to the others. "Hello everyone. I'm Ray, and this is my friend Tom. Tom's visiting from Oklahoma."

Murmurs of welcome rose, then faded as the mustached lecturer clapped his hands and made fast towards them. The faithful ebbed away discretely as the man introduced himself as Gale Banks, and with gentle gestures pushed them into the parlor across the hall. Ray glanced back into the chapel. Each person was sitting perfectly still, eyes locked on the empty lectern. Even Ward was motionless. It was a relief to leave them.

The second room had a tall, square velvet-draped table with several stools around it, and on the wall a large, hand-tinted portrait of Ruth clad in biblical robes. Banks settled himself directly beneath the picture, took a small, lidded basket from beneath the table and pushed it across towards Ray.

"Pardon the practicalities, but I believe that Ward told you about the cost for instruction."

"Yes, yes he did."

Tom patted Ray's hand. "Let me get this, man." He took the sheath of bills from his coat and fanned through them, then plucked two out and tucked them into the little basket.

"That's too much—" started Banks, but Tom shushed him.

"Consider it a contribution to your efforts. It's not every day I get the opportunity to support those who do God's work in fresh pastures. Now tell us about your very interesting sect. Do you meet often?"

Banks nodded agreeably. "We meet weekly here in town, but our members often go on retreat to enjoy a closer communion with the holy spirit. And each of us who joins up is given a daily spiritual practice by which to ring the bell for God."

"Was that what Ward was doing, when I met him on Wilshire?" suggested Ray.

"Yes. It's very peaceable, and makes the lessons clearer. She"—he cast a longing look up at Ruth, "has a gift for recognizing the voice within each of us that cries to come out. That's really what we're all about, gentlemen. We study and seek to become, each of us, more purely what we already are."

Tom made an appreciative noise, then half stood, holding his belly. "The toilet?"

"Right up the stairs, Mr. James. You all right?"

"Something's just disagreeing. Pardon me, Mr. Banks. Ray." As planned, he lurched from the room and bounded up the steps. The toilet door stood open at the front of the house, and he pulled it shut, then checked behind the other doors on the landing. A room with cheerful wallpaper suggesting it had once been a child's nursery, empty save for a table stacked with hundreds of pamphlets. A simple bedroom with a single bed in the center of the room, a table and a lamp. One door was locked.

Tom opened his billfold and slipped a narrow piece of metal from its sheath. One sharp push, another, and the lock gave. He stepped inside and pulled the door shut behind him. It was pitch black inside. He felt for a light switch.

Nothing. He stepped forward, into a thick curtain which he brushed aside. It was another bedroom, larger than the last. The only light came from the diamond shaped window in the walk-in closet.

His eyes adjusted. The room appeared to be some sort of shrine. Against the wall, inside a half moon of empty chairs, a day bed was heaped with quilts, framing the reclining figure of what he first took to be a small person, then recognized as a delicately smirking boudoir doll. Nearly life sized, its stuffed limbs tipped with splayed porcelain fingers peeped out from frilly white silk robes. The doll face was framed by curly golden hair. At the foot of the bed, fresh lilies were arranged in a funeral spray. He smelled incense, the flowers, and something cloying and unfamiliar.

On the table with the lilies was a small framed photo of a young girl. He took it over to the window. She was stunning. Arched brows over gentle, laughing eyes. Soft, round cheeks sliding gracefully to a pointed chin. Thick curls, brushed away from an intelligent brow. A cupid's bow mouth that seemed about to open in laughter.

Without thinking, he slipped the frame into his pocket.

He reset the lock, stepped quietly to the toilet and flushed, twice.

Returning to the parlor, he found Ray and Banks bent together over a sheet of paper. Banks had drawn a series of parallel lines, with stars at one end and blotches at the other, and was going over the lines to thicken them. The ink pooled under his fingers as he looked up and exclaimed, "So you see how obvious it is—and how marvelous!"

"Yes, yes. It really is fascinating. Tom, come here, look at this diagram. You see how there is a correlation between what exists in the sky and beneath the earth? These are deposits, Tom. Coal, gems, gold. Oil."

"Oil, eh? Well, I'm surely interested in anything concerning oil." Tom pulled up a stool and straddled it, cowboy style. "Are you saying there is a way to chart the stars and use that information to locate oil on earth?"

"There is going to be such a method, yes. The revelation is not complete, but as more formulas are revealed to our Mother May and Sister Ruth, they will complete their book, and then we will be able to find everything that is hidden. This knowledge will usher in a new era of prosperity and peace. We are all so excited—and so pleased to share the good news with new friends."

Tom pulled the inky paper close and studied it for a moment. "So, how can I get a copy of this book? When it's done, that is."

"All of our publications are by subscription. The first copies will go to members of our organization, and then later they will be made freely available throughout the earth."

"Yeah? And what's the cost of a subscription?"

Banks laughed.

"I don't know. It is different for everybody. Only Sister Ruth can tell you the cost of your subscription—that is, if you are interested in becoming one of us and supporting the Great Work."

"I'm interested. When can I meet this Sister Ruth?"

"Come back on Tuesday. She'll be here all day long. I'll tell her you're coming."

"I'll do that. Until then, Mr. Banks. Good-bye."

In the car, Ray laid his hat on his lap and shook his head, as if to clear the impressions out.

"Ugh. What a creepy crowd."

"You don't know the half of it. I let myself into a locked room upstairs. It's all laid out like a funeral for one of those French dolls the flappers cart around. Flowers, burning incense, chairs for visitors." He didn't mention the photo he'd taken. "Well, if nothing else, I've got a date to meet this taxi-dancing siren on Tuesday. That's something. Let's get out of here. I can't stand this street."

"It is a little down market, isn't it?"

"It's where that pig Hickman dumped Marion Parker's torso." Tom spat. "With her eyes sewn open so her father'd pay the ransom."

Ray remembered the notorious child kidnapping of two winters past, the manhunt and reward, the horrible discovery, the killer dragged back from Oregon by detectives who'd dropped him on his head a few times on the train home. Then the quick execution.

"You were there?"

"I was there. It's over. Forget it. What now?"

"We're pretty close to Dabney's house. Let's see how Alice is holding up, and find out where her husband's staying."

This time, Ray's rap was met with silence. He knocked again, put his mouth up to the milk chute and called "Alice, it's Ray Chandler. I know you're home. Open the door."

The knob turned, and Alice peeped out. Her eyes were mostly whites, and she was sweating. She saw Tom standing behind Ray and recoiled.

"Who's this man? I don't know him."

"My friend, Tom James. He's a policeman, Alice. We're here to help you. Open this door."

She stepped aside and the men entered. Alice wilted on the second step of the staircase, and began to sob. Her pajama top gaped open. Ray settled beside her, took her sideways in his arms and made soothing sounds. He put his coat across her shoulders. After a few moments, her sobs slowed. Ray led her to the kitchen table, and put the kettle on.

"First tea, then we'll talk. Just take your time. You can cry as long as you want."

"I don't want to cry. I want to die."

"Now now, that's a very silly thing to say. You know, I'm going to talk to your husband's uncle tomorrow, and get all this foolishness about your wardrobe straightened out. And then you'll be in the clover. So what have you got to cry about?"

"This!" She pulled a folded sheet of paper from her pajama top pocket, shoved it across the table and turned away in disgust.

Ray opened the note. Printed with the same mix of red and black ink as the pamphlets sold by Ward, it was a threat.

> DABNEY–Whosoever BETRAYS the confidence of the Divine Order of the Royal Arms of the Great Eleven shall be BROKEN as upon a wheel, his tongue BLISTERED, his fingers CURLED so no pen can rest between them. HONOR your promise to the holy ones, or FEAR will be your only companion until DEATH.

"Where did you get this, Alice?"

She stared ahead and whispered, "It was on Clifford's pillow when I woke up. Yesterday. I didn't sleep last night. Ray, I'm so scared. I've been thinking about things that I'd put out of my mind, and I don't like them at all."

93

Tom was turning the note over in his hands by the window. He tucked it into his coat. "We need to get her out of here. Take her someplace where nobody can find her. Muriel's not using her room at the Mayfair. Do you have the key?"

"Of course."

"Fine. We'll take her up the back steps. Mrs. Dabney, is there anything you want to bring with you? You may be away from home for a few days."

"Just a few little things, I guess."

"Ray, go with her and wait outside her bedroom. I'll keep watch down here."

"Okay."

"And hurry."

Alice Dabney sat in an armchair in Muriel's hotel suite. She was wearing brocaded slippers and a simple brown linen dress of Muriel's that Ray had assured her she was free to borrow, along with anything else in the closet. She was to keep the door bolted and chained, and not open it for anyone other than Tom or himself. The change of scene had calmed her somewhat, but she was still anxious and pale.

"Can you sleep?" Tom asked.

"Not now. I think I'll be able to in a little while. Once my heart stops pounding."

"Then let's talk about it now. Do you know who left this note in your bedroom?"

"Someone from our group. But you see, it could have been anyone. I don't lock the house."

"What is this confidence that can't be broken?"

"It's—it's complicated. I don't know if I should say. What if they find out I've spoken with you?"

"I'll protect you, Mrs. Dabney. The whole police force will. Threats are against the law, and nobody is going to get away with frightening you. Besides, your husband has already told us quite a bit about May and Ruth and their organization. It can only help if you fill in the parts we don't already know."

She was quiet for a long moment, looking down at the hands in her lap. The fingers of her left hand twined around her right, as though in combat. Her right hand formed a fist inside the cup of the left, then relaxed. She had made her decision, and when she spoke, she was calm and sure.

"It would take a long time to tell you everything. I'll tell you the important parts, and if you're confused, just stop and ask me to explain."

"Okay. Go on."

"Well, when Clifford and I married, we didn't have a church. We thought we'd try a few out and see where we felt at home. But, you see, we found that we felt at home trying a different faith each week, so for a long time we did that. It was very interesting. California has so many types of religion, doesn't it?"

"That's true. Go on."

"About five years ago, we heard about Mother May and Sister Ruth, and we went to see them up on Bunker Hill and hear about this angelic transcription. There was just a small group of believers then. We liked them so much we came back—first time we ever had. So that's how we came to be part of the group. You follow?"

"Mmm-hmm."

"Okay. Clifford had a special relationship with Mother May. They often talked alone together, about the Great Work and how he could become a keystone of the church. And I know that he thought if he could just use the secrets in the book for a few months before anyone else in the oil business saw it, that he could secure some leases so that we'd always be wealthy."

"This is the book that isn't finished yet?"

"That's right. It's the last number in the series—the biggest one—and it's just been a bear to complete. The angel has been quiet for some months, which has us all on edge.

Anyway, the book isn't just about where to find oil and gems and such. There's also the secret of how to bring the dead back to life, which you might know is a miracle, and something that did happen regularly in Bible days. Clifford was very interested in resurrection, in the idea of it. He told me that Mother May said when the work was done, he would have a new Concord, and that was to drive the resurrection engine."

"Concord—that's sort of his job within your faith?"

"Yes. We all have jobs. The resurrection engine, near as I can tell, is like a tractor with an organ on the back. It can smite people down, and then bring them back up again."

"You believed this? Clifford believed it?

"Maybe it's a metaphor. I'm sure I don't know. Clifford seems to believe it, but he talked much more with Mother May than I did. Anyway, those are the secrets of the book. Did Clifford tell you about Sammie Rizzio?"

"Rizzio—is that Ruth's husband? Where does he stay?"

"That's her husband. He's been gone a long time. Ruth said he left her, but I guess he must be dead. Mother May said he needed to renounce his unbelieving ways, and to dance at the mouth of the river, across the beach on poisoned sands. She had a druggist who used to come to our meetings make her the poison, and Sammie and they went down one night to make that Concord. He never did come back, and the druggist stopped coming around right after."

"You think Sammie Rizzio was murdered? Poisoned?"

"I didn't know what to think, except that it would be better if I didn't think much about it. Or to talk about it, either. I shouldn't be talking about it now."

She stared at her lap for a spell, then went on in a childish, sing-song voice. "Oh—another secret in the book is about healing. That's something Mother May and Sister Ruth already do. There was this lady, Frances. She was real sick. And they cured her, like you cure a piece of meat, inside an oven. I never saw this but I heard talk about it. This was up at Harmony Hamlet, in the hills. They say she was in this oven for two days, and then Mother May said everybody had to go to the beach to see the sun setting. And when they got back, Frances had got up and walked away, and we never saw her again."

She let out a dry snicker. "I guess she must dead, too. You must think I'm a prize fool."

"No, ma'am. I think you're a good person who was led astray. What was Sammie like?"

"Sammie? Good looking, with curly black hair and a big smile. Kind of excitable. He liked to do magic tricks."

"Tell me about Harmony Hamlet."

"Oh, that's just some land we bought. It's out in the Valley, almost to Ventura. We found it when Clifford was heading out to look at the wells for his uncle, and when Mother

May said it wasn't safe for everyone to stay in the city, we gave it to our friends to live on. Most of the members of our group live up there now, Mother May and Sister Ruth among them. I guess there must be seventy people now."

"But you and Clifford stayed in town?"

"Yes. They told us we weren't wanted there. Isn't that funny?"

"Sure, it's funny. Was this around the time you started feeling the pinch in your finances?"

"Clifford doesn't really talk to me about those things. Maybe—I don't know."

"All right, let's be sure I understand. This lady Frances and Sammie Rizzio have disappeared, and the pharmacist, too?"

"No, she just stopped coming to meetings. She's still got her store downtown. But there's someone else who went missing, a long time ago. That was Willa Rhoads, that pretty little girl. She was part of our group when we first began, sort of an assistant to Sister Ruth. Then she was just gone, and nobody would say a thing about it."

"Were her parents in the group, too?"

"Her foster parents, William and Martha. They still are. Yes, I guess I haven't seen her in four, five years. She'd be about twenty now."

"Do you think she might have run away?"

"Oh, no. She was devoted to her parents, and not worldly at all. I don't know what happened to her. One week she was there holding the curtains back before the altar, and the next time we came she was gone. Oh, I don't want to think about it any more! Do you think we'll be able to get on with our lives?"

"Sure you will. You're making a start just by talking about these things. I think we better go and talk with your husband, though—clarify some of the matters you weren't privy to. Where can we find him?"

"Clifford's at El Encanto. That's where he goes whenever his nerves are shot."

"Fine. Get some rest, Mrs. Dabney. We'll check in on you in the morning."

"Am I going to be safe here?"

"Absolutely safe," Tom told her.

"What a nice thought. I hope you're right about that. I will go to sleep now, I think."

"Good night, Mrs. Dabney. Sweet dreams."

In the hall, Tom said, "You were awfully quiet in there."

"Just letting you do your job."

"What do you think?"

"I think when Muriel calls next, I'm going to tell her to come on home."

"Good idea. Why don't you just go back to your place and wait on her call? I can see Dabney."

"Would you? I'd be grateful."

"Go."

Eight

But Muriel didn't phone. She woke in her cottage, stiff from the hours standing at the conveyor belt, and yet bursting with energy. It was only eight and the air was already stifling. Her clean dress, flapping in the window, was dry now, and even before getting up she decided she'd go to the sea today. In the bath, she soaped up the edge of the towel, scrubbed the dry black walnut stains from her fingers, and thanked God for Sunday. It was, she realized, the first Sunday in months that she hadn't been drunk the night before.

The canyon road was winding and narrow, with steep drops beyond gravel turnouts. After one frightening lurch when she became distracted wondering what Ray was doing, she forced herself to focus only on the car and the road ahead, and when the blue horizon opened up beneath her, with whitecaps and distant island peaks, it seemed like a fairy tale reward.

Turning north, she savored the cool, salty wind, although it was soon replaced by hot blasts stale with steer manure. The farms of Oxnard spread across the plain, empty but for the occasional water tank or parked tractor, and then the sea was at her left again.

At Ventura, she crossed the railroad tracks and parked among all the other cars at the edge of the sand. The hulking white bath house stood by the long pier, its flanks pierced with squat arcades. On the roof, a lonesome red pennant snapped in the breeze. The beach was crowded, and a steady stream of people moved between the bath house and the shore. Inside, she paid a dime to rent a swimsuit and towel and changed in the women's dressing room.

It felt good to be anonymous in a crowd, just another warm young body slipping out of her street clothing and into the neutral uniform of physical culture. The dark wool suit was tight at the shoulders, and she tugged at it there, then pulled the bottom down to the center of her thighs.

The big bath house hummed with conversation. Upstairs, older folks sat with their elbows resting on the wooden railing, faces shadowed under hats. The partial skylight dappled the great saltwater plunge, and in the water, children and young adults splashed and swam in its warm rays.

Occasionally, somebody would climb to the top of the two-story slide and slip into the water with a shriek. Muriel

103

dove in and swam a few laps, but the crowding made it impossible to maintain a pace, and soon she resigned herself to floating upright in place, kicking and stroking the water in neat figure-eights.

Tired then, she floated easily on her back with her eyes closed, and felt the tension of the past days slip out of her neck. She didn't think about Ray, or the Dabneys, or grade AA walnuts or mysterious women in the hills. She didn't think about how long it had been since she wrote to her parents. She didn't think about Los Angeles or marriage or children. She thought only of the salty water on her skin, the happy voices in the air, and the sun warm on her face.

She left the pool and went out the big doors onto the beach, found an empty bit of sand and laid down on her towel. It was hot, luxurious. She dozed off, and when she woke fell into conversation with the girl beside her. Lillian Potter was home from nursing college in San Francisco, and spending the summer helping her mother out with the new baby, a girl. Out of politeness more than any real interest, Muriel expressed a general affection for small children, and Lillian invited her back to her family's house for lunch and to meet the baby.

It felt nice to be around a girl her own age and to sit down with ordinary folks to eat a meal. Mrs. Potter had baked a chicken and it sat steaming on the tray at the sink's edge as she used the big spoon to set little carrots and gravy and dumplings all around it. She seemed happy to meet Muriel and didn't begrudge the extra appetite.

The baby was napping, and the girls tiptoed into the nursery and peeped at her in her crib. She had curly brown hair and fat fists thrown back over her shoulders. She smelled nice.

Her sister leaned in close and whispered "Little Flora, are you sleepy?"

The baby burbled and smiled without waking. Lace curtains filtered the mid-day light and cast spider web patterns on pale grey walls.

Muriel had a strange impression that the room had always been there and would never change, that little Flora would not wake up or grow, but just lay there smiling and responding to loving voices in her subtle way.

She excused herself to the washroom, where she splashed her face with cold water and stared at her own clean, freckled face for a long time before pulling herself together and walking out to meet her new friends.

The course of the conversation was predictable, yet without even planning it, Muriel skipped back to the previous fall and said things about herself which would have been true then, but which were no longer true. In the picture she painted she was still a single girl, working in the Witmer

Brothers' offices as receptionist to Pat Connor, a fat, pushy property manager who was annoying but not dangerous. She had not yet encountered Ray Chandler in Pershing Square, or confided in him, or accepted his offer to find her better employment with his firm, higher up in the Giannini Building.

That was before she allowed him to seduce her with promises of love and excitement, before she left her small but pretty room on Bellevue for the hotel suite Ray rented, before the first time she stayed up with him until 5 in the morning, standing up in front of the window because he swore if she left him, or slept, or stopped listening, he would surely jump.

She talked about a life that had been hers as recently as November, and was shocked by how distant it felt.

She told her lies and ate the good wholesome food, then went downtown with Lillian and strolled along the boulevard where she bought a pair of sturdy, plain $2 shoes for work. Later, driving back towards her lonesome motel bed with Lillian's school address folded in her handbag and half a peach pie in brown paper on the seat beside her, she thought she really could have said she'd had a lovely time today, if only she could shake the feeling of being ashamed.

Nine

Ray stood on the sidewalk, looking up at his apartment.

The windows were shut despite the heat and the heavy curtains drawn tight. He could feel Cissy's simmering anger through the walls. Maybe she was in the cold bath that she kept always filled, with the basket of her things set on the side. He'd taken to showering at the club, or in Muriel's room, as less and less of the apartment was open to him. The fear of walking up those steps, opening the door and stepping into the hot, hostile space held him in place.

He pictured the heavy black telephone tucked into its little nook between the front room and the hall that led back to their bedrooms, the pencil stub and stack of folded foolscap paper beside it. Muriel's lifeline. He should be there. A man shouldn't dread going home. He wondered, briefly, if he would hear the phone ringing and have time to answer it, if he just waited out on the balcony where she couldn't see him.

Stupid idea. Idiotic. He squared his shoulders and trudged up the walk, up the steps. The apartment was as he expected, stale and dark, silent, with every door shut. He switched the hall light on. The telephone was off the hook. He put it back in its cradle. He looked down the hall towards his wife's room, and turned away.

He went into his office, checked his desk for messages— no, none—opened the window, then sank into the leather chair by the bookcase. His head felt like it was stuffed with sand. He wondered if this was how he would live for the rest of his life, unwelcome, wincing against an assault which might or might not come. He wondered how long that life would be, and if the end would be painful or completely without feeling. He wondered if Cissy would leave her room today, and if she did, if she'd be silent or explosively loud.

He closed his eyes.

A man shouldn't dread going home.

Ten

If it was hot in Los Angeles, it was stifling in Pasadena. Clots of still, brownish air clung fast to the foothills, and women swooned in bedrooms with damp towels on their faces. El Encanto was sleepy under old trees. An elderly gardener was crouched in the shade of a mock-Tudor arch, pretending to weed. The gold sign on the half glass door of the administration building observed that this was private property and permission to enter could be revoked at any time. Tom stepped inside, hoping for cooler air. He was disappointed. Behind the desk, a stout young woman with a red face under a wilted white cap looked up through piggy eyes.

"Yeah?"

"I'd like to see Clifford Dabney. He's a patient of yours."

"Is he now?" She managed to sound at once petulant and remote.

"He is. Now. And I'd like to see him. Now. Will you call him?"

"Well, assuming Mr. Clifford Dabney were a patient, which I am not saying he is or isn't, today is Sunday. And Dr. Cravens has given strict orders that we're to have no visitors on a Sunday. Didn't you see the sign?"

"It doesn't say anything about Sundays."

"It says the right to enter is revocable. Scram, buster. Try us again tomorrow. Maybe you'll get lucky."

"Will you be here tomorrow?"

"Nah."

"I feel luckier already."

El Encanto was the place that you went if you were a movie actress who couldn't keep from eating bonbons, or a company president who drank himself into malnourishment on the eve of a public offering. Debutantes who started crying and didn't stop knew its leafy pathways well.

Its physician-managers understood the stresses of modern life, and had tools for untangling them, leaving its guests slim, calm and sober—eventually, and at significant expense.

Tom had been out here himself not too many months before, at the mayor's direction, to see the heiress wife of a playboy police captain who'd taken a marital elbow to the jaw in a car outside a Sunset Boulevard restaurant. She hadn't been in any condition to talk, but had written some colorful statements on the back of a magazine. He knew that the private patients could be found in bungalows away from the main buildings, and that for a few bucks most of the attendants could be convinced to head slowly back the way they came to retrieve something left off the supply cart. The guards were fat old Glendale cops who didn't want to be heroes.

Sunday was good as any other day.

Tom pulled out of the wide drive and circled the block. The front of the compound was ringed with a tall iron fence, but around the back untrimmed hedges were pocked by dead patches where animals and desperate patients traveled in their essential duties.

He slipped through an opening near the southeast corner and found himself beside a dilapidated shed. The door was open and the interior stacked high with old wheelchairs, firewood and battered trunks. More firewood was piled up on the cracked asphalt. Somewhere not close, he heard the thwack of a tennis ball, and a man cursing.

The grounds were very green and very still. Wide lawns dotted with stands of ferns and redwoods sprawled out towards the mountains, while winding paths connected a dozen neat bungalows. At the front of the property, through the trees, an L-shaped network of two-story stucco and wood buildings in the Arts & Crafts style served as administration and hospital quarters. It was from here that he'd come, dismissed by the receptionist.

Tom strolled purposefully among the bungalows. To the right of each door, an embossed ivory card set in a dark metal frame gave the first initial and last name of the patient in residence. Most doors were open for whatever breeze came, and through the screens he got the impression of dark, still spaces with silent figures somewhere within. He didn't see anybody moving.

At the eighth bungalow, he found his man. This door was closed. Tom knocked, got no answer, and turned the knob.

It was dark inside, with the neutral smell of a hired room. Thin electric light filtered in from the bathroom. A slim, dark-haired man in a bathrobe sat in the corner in an arm-chair, slippered feet on the ottoman. Despite the heat, he had a blanket over his shoulders. He smiled at Tom.

"Dabney?"

"Mmm-hmm. Maybe. Who wants to know?"

"I do. I'm working with Ray Chandler on his investigation of your financial losses. I've just got a couple of questions that need straightening out. Got a minute?"

"All right. Thank you so much." He didn't offer Tom a seat, or move to turn on a light. There was an awkward pause. Tom pushed the rumpled coverlet aside and sat on the sheeted bed. He pulled out his notebook.

"Your wife got a visit from your former business partners."

"Oh. Did she?"

"She's frightened."

"Frightened? No, I don't think so."

Dabney's lack of affect was troubling. Tom wondered if the man was quite right in the head.

"Anyway, she's safe now, so you don't need to worry."

"I never worry." He smiled and wrapped his blanket close.

"No? Imagine that. Right, let's get this business over with. Sammie Rizzio—what can you tell me about him?"

"He went away. Oh, a long time back."

"Willa Rhoads?"

"She went away, too."

"They just went away? Did they go someplace in particular? Did they leave together?"

"I don't remember what happens to people. They didn't matter to me." Dabney was, it seemed, capable of mild irritation. Tom decided not to push the matter.

"How about Harmony Hamlet?"

The question sparked his interest. He leaned forward, slightly. "Very pretty place. I'd like to build a lodge out there, when my circumstances are improved. Put in a corral for horses, sink a well, maybe a swimming pool for the summer. It does get hot out in the valley."

"Where is Harmony Hamlet? If I wanted to go up and take a look, I'd drive—?"

"Well, you'd take the Cahuenga Pass out of L.A. Bring lots of water for the ride. Or you can buy oranges on the way. Then up around Chatsworth you head out on the old pass. Then you want to start looking for the turn off. It's not marked, so—"

There was a sharp knock at the door, and a woman's voice called "Mr. Dabney, time for your medicine. You decent, hon?" The two men exchanged looks, Dabney's half a beat too slow. Tom lifted his fingers to his lips and stepped into the bathroom and behind the half-open door.

Dabney trilled, "I am utterly decent." Through the crack, Tom watched a slim blonde nurse cross the room, murmur something maternal to her patient and rustle at his clothing. Dabney clutched her white rump, grunted, then sighed a long "Thank you, baby doll." The nurse left. Tom stepped back into the room. Dabney was slumped back in his chair, eyes at half-mast. He didn't react to Tom's return.

"Hey. Dabney?"

Nothing.

Tom passed his hand before the man's eyes. A double puff of air from pursed lips, a giggle. Then, apparently, sleep.

An empty hypodermic needle rattled in the waste bin. This was the sort of rest cure that ensured worries stayed far away, and that Sunday staff wages were cheap. The room was empty of personal items. Dabney would be out for hours. There was no point in staying. The whole trip had been a waste of time. Tom fought back the sudden urge to hurt the sleeper, to pinch him somewhere where the skin was thin and leave a nasty welt to remember his visit by. He hated his own sadism, and wondered if he'd always be able to hold it back. It was why he didn't drink, not now. It was why he'd tucked himself up under Allie's wing in the first place.

He pinched himself instead, and the anger seeped away, only to be replaced by loneliness. He went downtown to lose himself among strangers. It was the only thing that could quiet his mind when he fought with himself this way.

Main Street was loud and crass in the late afternoon sun and smelled like hamburgers. Tom fell into a stroller's pace, observing the changing scene, not as a cop but as just a set of eyes, with the same cool detachment with which he'd watch the slim, darting bodies in a fish tank. It was restful to be just one conscious form among thousands on the sidewalk, wanting nothing that anyone was selling.

Main Street was a base and ugly boulevard, the end of the line. Lusts were whipped to a frenzy in its fleshpots, but rarely ever satisfied. Yawning thirsts were quenched in its rum cellars, only to grow back stronger with the dawn. Pawnbrokers promised cash for memories, never telling their customers that if they managed to redeem the shelved treasures they'd seem tawdry and pathetic upon collection.

Main Street was bright lights and hollering barkers, sharp-eyed women whose high color signified not youth but some tubercular condition, fat men who made thin men work hard for small wages, a place where boys were corrupted and girls ruined, where street preachers failed consistently to save souls, and where each one of these small tragedies meant nothing much at all.

Just inside the penny arcade across from the rescue mission, a couple of kids with dirty peach fuzz mustaches lurked around the peep booth. One idly turned the crank and snapped the gum in his mouth. A horn-shaped speaker blared a low-down blues. Inside her glass cage, the mechanical gypsy rolled her eyes and fanned five cards, waiting for a customer.

The crimes of Main Street were minor, tedious. A drunk sailor losing his roll to a B-girl, a newsboy hocking stolen watches, a vicious fight over a woman neither combatant cared one fig about. Occasionally, something unusual would happen—a murder or a lost child found—but on Main Street even a miracle would seem drab. Such was the klieg light power of the commercial engine that fed the place, and the artifice that was its only real product.

On Main Street, even the Salvation Army majors were blasé.

A skinny white fellow in a Hindu costume hopped around the sidewalk at 5th & Main. He had a banjo on a strap around his neck, but couldn't be bothered pluck it. On reaching the corner he threw back his head and bellowed, "See the geek! Genuine freak of nature and a marvel to behold, only at The World Museum!"

Here, people were just characters playing at their two-dimensional roles: the whore, the john, the hustler, the mark, the pimp, the bum, the temperance worker, the loan shark, the addict, the wide-eyed boy from Beaver Dam, Kentucky, who came to Los Angeles and had all his dreams dashed and then remade again into something more practical, less likely to be dashed again.

Signs covered every permanent surface, a cacophony of typography and misused punctuation.

WE BUY GOLD.

5¢ HOURLY SHOWS ALL DAY

SEE! A REAL MUMMY

GOING OUT OF BUSINESS - EVERY THING MUST GO

ROOMS - FIRE PROOF

A boy walked against traffic in the gutter. He was pulling a narrow cart with an upright painted sign advertising the coming of the circus, featuring Goliath (the mammoth sea elephant, one ton heavier than last season), and Hugo

Zacchini, human cannonball. The kid's shoes were falling apart at the back, and the skin of his heels stained black.

Tom stepped into a narrow flower shop, turning sideways to pass the sprawling sprays of moist, wilting roses standing on mirrored shelves. There was nobody behind the counter. He lifted the little trap, pushed the sleazy curtain aside, and walked down the steep basement steps. He tasted violet perfume on the smoky air.

Down below, a radio was playing soft classical music, and three little gals in tight satin dresses were slouched on their bar stools. When they heard his steps on the stone, they pulled their stomachs in. The blonde at the end looked over her shoulder, made Tom for a cop and clucked disapprovingly. She yawned at him. The bartender gave him the fish eye. It wasn't Friday, and he wasn't the designated collector.

Tom shrugged and took a seat in the corner. The girls slumped down again. It was peaceful down here, with the music and the cool stone wall against his back.

A little time passed. A soft-looking guy in a wilted linen suit came downstairs and admired the scenery. He went up to the blond and whispered something to her. She snuggled up close and called for a champagne cocktail and a bourbon, water back. You'd have to be fresh off the truck not to know that her $2 drink was nothing but ginger ale with a sugar cube and a dash of bitters, and that the bourbon box behind the bar still had Venice Beach sand between the slats. She held the mark's hand with a practiced tenderness, and drank her cocktail fast enough to keep the boss happy, but not so fast that the man beside her felt like a fool.

It was illegal as hell, but almost innocent compared to most of what went on above and below Main Street. The blond whispered in the soft man's ear and he traced the curve of her jaw with the edge of his thumb. Tom supposed there wasn't much harm in it, but he felt all of a sudden mad and a little sick and he made for the stairs. It wasn't worth fighting them. He didn't care so much as all that.

Main Street was an education in the real life of humans. Books were full of remote ideals that couldn't be realized in everyday life except by those insulated from reality by money, breeding and character. The people you met in church were wearing their best faces. Down here, nobody pretended to be something they weren't. It wasn't a pleasant world, but it was a natural one. Since he'd first arrived in Los Angeles, Tom had been coming here to practice compassion. He tried to love everyone, but it was hard. At his best, he managed not to judge.

But he wasn't at his best today.

Eleven

The conveyor belt was made of unbleached sailcloth which had turned brownish tan from the years' accumulation of walnut dust and dirty fingers. It had a rough mend in bright red thread that Muriel looked forward to seeing each time it crossed her station. The conveyor belt took three minutes and forty seconds to make a circuit of the packing house. On her second day working, she played a game with herself, trying to anticipate the arrival of the mend without looking left for it, counting down in her head, three-two-one-now! She considered herself a winner if the mend was no more than five women away. For each time she won, she promised herself a ticket to the Philharmonic. By mid-day, she'd won twice.

In a part of her brain not playing the game, she was thinking about how to ingratiate herself further to the cult ladies. She'd picked up a box of fudge at the drugstore in town, and figured she'd offer that as a thank you for Saturday's

120

supper. As to how to get them talking, that would have to come naturally.

Gradually, she became aware that the cult ladies were watching her. She felt their eyes on her skin like soft puffs. Glancing over, she saw that they were huddled together, whispering. Then a red-cheeked, motherly one called Anna darted out of the crowd and to her station. She had a soft voice with a slight Scandinavian accent. "Say, can I talk to you for a minute?"

"Sure, okay." Muriel shook her half-full nut box down, and tucked it under the shelf. She caught the forewoman's eye, held her palm up and mouthed, "Five minutes." The forewoman shrugged. Muriel and Anna walked out to the dinner tree and sat at the bench.

"What's doing?"

"Well," Anna drawled, "We was just wondering, where d'you come from?"

"Julian, down San Diego way. You?"

"Sweden, but Oregon, really. And are you traveling, or looking to stay?"

"I don't quite know. My folks are all gone now. Guess I'm just trying to find my feet. What about you? Do you stay with your folks?"

"I stay with my chosen family. My folks are gone, too. That's your car out there, right?"

"Sure thing, that's my car. Say, what's this about, Anna?"

"I'm asking about you because we think you might be selected."

"Selected?"

"Uh-huh. Somebody is supposed to come here with a car, and we're wondering if that's you. Ruth said they were coming, with a nice car."

"Gee, I dunno. My car is pretty nice, as cars go. How would I know if I were selected?"

"That's something Ruth would know. Would you like to come up to the camp later on and meet her? You can see where we live. It's awful nice. You can show your car to Ruth. And if it turns out you are the one that's selected, I bet you can stay for services and supper. What do you say?"

"That sounds real fine, Anna. I'd be happy to come visit. Just give me the directions, and I'll change and ride up after work."

But Anna just smiled. "I better ride up with you. We don't get a lot of visitors, and it's kind of hard to find."

"Okay. After work, then."

Tamping down the urge to grin, Muriel went back to the line.

The ringing office phone startled Ray, and he stubbed his pen out into an angry blot, cracking the nib.

He'd been drawing a diagram on a sheet of blotter paper. The financial entanglements of Dabney and the cult leaders were a masterpiece of misdirection. Numerous firms had been incorporated, merged, dissolved and resumed. Some had names that were nearly identical, with the only change the doubling of unnecessary consonants or the addition of articles of speech. Nebulous real property was passed willy-nilly between the firms, described weirdly as "box of crazy quilts" or "spices, jars and associated packaging." Officers changed position. Mailing addresses varied by single digits. No clear declaration of business purpose was ever made, despite reams of double talk and legalese.

It was, in short, the most convoluted lot of nonsense that he'd seen in all his years in business. It hurt his head and made him wonder if the whole thing wasn't the old man's idea of a bad joke. But of course the old man didn't have a sense of humor, neither good nor bad.

Muriel's voice came down the crackly line.

"Hello, hello—is that you, Ray?"

He held the cold receiver tight against his face as if it were her hand. "Yes, I'm here. Where are you? Are you all right, dear?"

"I'm still in Chatsworth, I'm fine. Listen, I—"

"No, you listen—you need to come home right now."

"Home? No, listen—I've done it—I've got an invitation to Harmony Hamlet—"

"Muriel! You need to come home. The assignment is off. I need your help back at the office."

"Okay! Tomorrow! Anyway, I have to run, because she's waiting for me. Kiss kiss—"

"No—wait!" He realized he was talking down an empty line, and his voice dropped to a whisper. "I'm frightened for you."

He charged down the hall and stood hopping outside the elevator, struggling to pull his seersucker jacket over rolled shirtsleeves.

"Come on, come on, damn it."

He pushed the bell again. The elevator came. He grunted "ground" and turned away from the operator, behavior so atypically rude that it took a good ten seconds before the rattled man engaged the machine and set it on its course.

He was out before the cage stopped moving, through the tall bank doors, veering left and jogging down Seventh Street with his arms out in football tackle position, ready to push aside anyone who blocked his passage. But the crowds parted before him as if they sensed his reckless energy.

Tom was leaning against the lamppost at his station, talking with some red-headed hick. Ray grabbed his elbow and tugged. Tom wheeled around, fists ready, and saw it was his friend, pale, sweat-drenched and panting.

"I need you—Muriel—she's gone up there—we have to–"

Tom spoke as if to an animal in frenzy. "Okay, okay, easy now, okay." He turned from the stranger with an automatic apology, took Ray's arm and walked him back the way he'd come. At St. Vincent Court, he led him into the alley. It was cool there in the shadows of the buildings, away from the press of people. Ray, unused to so much exercise, buckled and sank to the ground. He wheezed and coughed, and cursed at himself.

Tom waited. Ray rose, mopped his face with his handkerchief, and delivered his burden.

"Muriel called. I told her to come home. I couldn't convince her. She's gone to Harmony Hamlet. She wouldn't listen. We have to save her."

"Okay."

"Now!"

"Yes, fine. Come on, we'll take my car."

"But Tom. But Tom. How are we going to find her?"

"We'll take Dabney with us."

"Oh. Of course. But Tom. But Tom."

"What is it, Ray?"

"I just want you to know that if anything happens to her I'm going to throw myself off a roof."

"Shut up, Ray. Stand here and don't move. I'll be back soon."

At his corner, Tom unlocked the call box and spoke down the open line.

"Hi, who is this? Oh, hello Lois. Badge 1828 here... Listen, honey, I've got the trots something fierce... Yeah, isn't it? Clock me out for the afternoon and send somebody down to mind the store, willya?... Yeah, I will. You too, thanks."

He shot a glance over his station, at the careless rubes stepping out in front of death machines with their eyes on women's rumps, the greasy smear of some unknown unguent on the curb in front of the bank, the jerky newsboy who would start practicing his pickpocket routine the minute he walked away.

He thought about staying put until his relief came. But his sick call depended on him not being here when help arrived, and anyway, the way things were at headquarters, it could be hours before another cop took his spot. Wishing his people safe passage, he returned to his anxious friend in the alleyway.

On the drive out to Pasadena, Ray talked. He didn't make a lot of sense. He talked about Muriel's favorite foods to order in restaurants, and about the time she'd insisted he let her into a house he was looking after for a production engineer colleague who was drilling in Mexico, and how she'd begged him to let her cook them a meal in the kitchen and he'd refused her.

He'd been less scrupulous about his colleague's bed, but he didn't mention that fact.

He talked about his marriage, female moods, and how long it had been since he and Cissy had slept in the same bed. He started to talk about his war service, then he stopped and was quiet for a long time, and Tom thought he wasn't going to say anything else, and then he said, "It might have been better for everyone if I hadn't made it back."

After that he did stop talking. Tom felt a chill, and kept trying to think of something to say, but there wasn't anything in his arsenal that would have been suitable, so instead of talking he started to sing. He sang a folk song that was popular with the old fellows who sat up all day on the porch of the store in Beaver Dam, where he'd been a boy. It was a ballad about a girl named Omie who went down to the river with her lover, but her lover came back alone. He had killed her.

He didn't know why he wanted to sing that weird old song, except that the melody of it always gave him a chill somewhat like the feeling he had listening to Ray talk about his troubles. And also, he couldn't stand the silence with that thought dying on the air.

The song ended, but the last note seemed to linger for a long time. Ray smiled.

"That was nice. You don't often hear that kind of music in California. It reminds me of England."

"Kentucky is a lot like England, they say."

"Kentucky! Everyone's the same everywhere, I guess."

"I've been meaning to ask you, how you came to be in the oil business. Not many Englishmen in oil."

"I'm not English, though—I'm from Chicago. And as for oil, I came to it through the milk trade. I made friends from Los Angeles, oil people as it happens, when I was younger. They recommended me to the Los Angeles Creamery, and I helped manage that office for some years, in the city and up north. Dabney was near by, and my friends thought it couldn't hurt to have me in the room making certain nothing happened that they didn't know about, so I made the leap. Oil's bad enough, but milk is filthy. I was glad to be done with it.

"How's milk filthy?"

"How isn't it? Don't touch the stuff, if you're smart. D'you recall the name George Platt?"

"Can't say I do."

"Before your time, I suppose. When I began working for Platt, he'd just been found guilty of selling condensed milk mixed with the regular variety and calling it cream.

That was hardly the foulest stuff we sold under the cream label, but that's what they nabbed him on, and it made the papers. Of course, it was simply a matter of not looking after the inspectors, an error not repeated on my watch. Platt had bigger problems, though."

"How so?"

"It's always real estate, isn't it? Some large bit of ranch land was acquired for the expansion of the business, and there was a man called Deyoe who believed he was entitled to a commission on the transaction. Platt disagreed. This Deyoe called at the office repeatedly, making some terrible scenes, until I brought in a big man to sit in the corner and wait for him. He didn't come again after that, but he was still aggrieved. Platt thought it was all done with, but it wasn't done in Deyoe's mind. I think it must have driven him a bit mad."

"What happened?"

"Platt was stupid. After all this, he accepted a ride in to work from Deyoe, God knows why. They argued on the drive, and Deyoe took out a little gun and shot Platt in the back. He thought he'd killed him, and he blew his own brains out there on the road. But my man Platt was only playing dead, and was well enough in the hospital to tell reporters that his assailant was a lunatic."

"So. Where'd all this happen?"

"Sixth, at Catalina. I often ride by and think about old Platt. He was a brute and a bore, but he taught me a great deal about business."

"Do you think he cheated Deyoe?"

Ray laced his fingers together and was quiet for a moment. "For the longest time I didn't. Our books looked clean, and the old man always professed his innocence. But I found some odd documents tucked away that told a different story, or hinted at one." He sighed. "Maybe it doesn't matter what really happened. Platt got his land, Deyoe got his revenge, and I got my education."

"And the citizens got good, wholesome milk to drink."

"Oh yes. Full of healthful calcium to make strong bones." Ray grimaced. "I prefer oil. It doesn't pretend to be anything but nasty stuff, flammable and greasy. Foul-smelling. It suits me."

When they got to El Encanto, Tom drove slowly around the property and explained the role Ray was to play inside. He parked behind the broken hedge. From the trunk, Tom took two lengths of strong cord, a pair of handcuffs, a wool blanket and his revolver in its holster. He clipped the handcuffs to his belt, strapped his holster on, stowed the gun and buttoned his coat. He put the rope in his pocket, folded the blanket and hung it over Ray's arm. They slipped sideways through the green wall and onto the hospital grounds.

Tom went into the shed and found a wheelchair that rolled. He brushed dust and cobwebs off with his hands. Ray sat down, pulled his hat low and draped the blanket over his knees. Tom shook his head. It looked wrong. Ray got up again.

Tom pushed the empty chair along the winding path, walking fast, Ray close behind. He scanned the property for movement. All was quiet. An orderly pushed a wheeled cart around the corner of the administration building. Through an open window, classical music played. There was nobody around the bungalows. Dabney's was shut up tight. Tom pushed the chair behind a stand of ferns, tried the knob, turned it, and the two men ducked inside.

Dabney was on the bed, drugged. Tom went over and slapped his face lightly. A weak groan. He slapped harder and called the man's name. Dabney started coming around.

Tom turned to Ray. "Find his clothes. Then get the chair."

They sat him up on the edge of the bed and dressed him. Dabney slipped in and out of his daze. One minute he was asking Ray what he wanted, the next he was smiling foolishly, his eyes tracking some invisible flying thing near the ceiling. When they stood him up, he wobbled. Tom took one of the lengths of rope and looped it around Dabney's waist. He tied him into the wheelchair, arranged the blanket around his hips, and went to the window. He pried the blinds apart, scanned the grounds, and directed Ray to push the chair.

Bearing Dabney's limp weight, the old wheelchair revealed the reason it had been banished to the shed. The right wheel was warped, and it took all Ray's strength to keep it rolling. The trip across the campus seemed interminable, and Ray felt horribly exposed. He braced himself to start running if anyone challenged them.

But nobody noticed.

The weird little party reached the shed. Tom untied Dabney. Limp, eyes closed, he couldn't stand. Tom sent the wheelchair flying with a kick and tossed Dabney over his shoulder. They pressed back through the bushes, poured the drugged man into the backseat, and were soon on the highway, bound for the place where secrets went to hide.

Twelve

Muriel put the phone on the hook and peeped through the folding window. Anna was leaning against the wall by the newsstand, leafing through a magazine. The kid was polishing glasses behind the soda counter. The ceiling fan spun fast, its long cord whipping like a slow snake between the aisles. Flypaper swayed, too.

Muriel felt excited, but also calm. It was as if she could see herself from outside—a young woman skilled in lies and deferred desires, playing a role within another. Wherever she was going now, she was on her way.

Ray said he wanted her to come back, but she didn't believe him. She wasn't certain she wanted to come back, not to where she'd been. If she could return to Los Angeles with the key to Clifford Dabney's lost assets, maybe she'd write her own memo in Ray's signature style and send it straight to the old man—only with her name on the line that said "from."

133

Let Ray fritter his days away in Los Angeles, doing whatever it was he did there. She was the one who'd seized the moment and tracked the criminals to their lair, who'd gained their trust, who wasn't afraid to go up alone to meet them.

Or if she was a little bit afraid, it wasn't so much that she'd let it stop her. She felt certain, for the first time in a long while, that she was where she wanted to be.

Anna was wearing a funny little cap, too small for her head, green velvet with a double row of little cream colored buttons in a running pattern around the edge. It seemed impossible to see anything sinister in a person who could have chosen or worn such a cap. Muriel fixed her own neat hair, patted her dress down where it had caught at her hips, and walked out into the store.

"Thanks for waiting. Was there anything you needed before we got back on the road? Powder room?"

"I'm fine, thank you. Did you talk to your doctor?"

"No, he's gone for the afternoon. I got his nurse. I'll try again tomorrow. It's nothing serious, nothing that can't wait."

At San Fernando, Tom stopped at a hamburger joint and got some coffee and donuts in a sack. He told Ray to take the wheel, and got into the back with Dabney. The drugged

134

man had been slumped against the window, but Tom pulled him upright and sat close so he couldn't tip over. He held the waxed cup under Dabney's nose and slowly poured the hot dark fluid into his mouth. Dabney choked and sputtered. Tom waited for him to stop, and resumed the process. Ray drove on, fast and quiet.

The coffee and time had the desired effects, and as the shadows lengthened across the valley floor, Dabney's slack face rearranged itself in a pattern of awareness. He wiggled uncomfortably against the body tight against his flank, and Tom moved to the other side of the car. Dabney remained upright. It was time to start talking.

Dabney began. "Chandler, is that you up there?"

"It's me."

"What's going on?"

"I'm driving. Don't bother me. Talk to him."

He looked at Tom. "I know you. Where do I know you from?"

"I visited you at El Encanto. Remember? We talked about your wife."

"Yes, that's right. How is Alice? Is she enjoying her solitude?"

"Alice is fine. We're not going to talk about Alice. You're going to answer my questions, Clifford. All of them."

Tom stared at Dabney in the way he'd been taught by a cop called Brinnegar, who was dead now.

"Imagine," Brinnegar had told him, "that your suspect is made of meat, that he's sitting in the butcher's window, and beginning to spoil."

The involuntary flare of disgust across Tom's face shook Dabney, who was accustomed to deference from his social inferiors. But like most men with inherited wealth and no accomplishments of their own, he was at his core insecure and slipped neatly into subservience, just as Tom had told Ray he would.

"Oh. What is it you wish to know?"

"First off, where's Harmony Hamlet?"

"Out by the Ventura wells, in the country—"

"No, stupid. Where precisely is Harmony Hamlet? Right now we are on the Devonshire road, heading towards the Santa Susana Pass. When we get there, what road do we take?"

"It's a little road. It doesn't have a name. But I'll show you."

"Good. How much did the land cost?"

"Can I sit up front with Ray?"

"No. How much did it cost, Clifford?"

Dabney made a sniveling noise, then answered in a soft voice. "Well, there are two parts of it. The bit Alice and I

136

bought when we were first married, that was about $5,000. That's down in the valley, by the stream. And the bigger part, where the caves and the flat top are, that was $9,000. No, $9,300."

"Good. Now I want you to describe this place, starting from the road in and including every building and every person on the land. Don't skip a thing." Tom took a donut out of the sack and ate it in three bites. He didn't offer one to Dabney.

"Can I have something to eat?"

"Maybe, if I like your answers. So get talking."

Dabney described the narrow gravel road lined with oaks, which curled around the stream and up into the mountains. He told Tom about the flat, treeless half-mile stretch that made it impossible to sneak up on the encampment. Small paths led away from the road in this section, with the abandoned rusting automobiles of cult members run off into gullies.

Halfway up the hill, the cottages began, a smattering of modest two- and three-room wooden structures, each with a sleeping porch sheltered by a canvas wall and roof. Behind the buildings were vegetable gardens. On the eastern edge of the property there was a barn and several animal pens. The cultists kept pigs, chickens, ducks, mules, goats and horses.

At the top of the rise, one of the cottages was bigger than the others: two stories with a proper porch, sparkling cut glass in the windows, and fresh paint on the clapboard siding. This was where Mother lived with her immediate family, and whichever member of the group was currently in favor as a servant. He admitted he'd never been invited inside.

Windowless, stucco wings that looked as if they had been hewn out of the mountain swept out to either side. These were chapels, each with a giant central door that reached nearly to the flat roof-line. These wings were painted dark indigo blue, with golden stars scattered over the walls. They were built flush against the hillside, a protected space in which the believers could practice their rites and study the teachings provided by angels—or so Ruth and Mother said.

As for the small cottages, these were home to believers, most of them older women with small incomes that they turned over to the organization.

"Any men?"

"Of course. There's Gale Banks, he's Mother's secretary, I suppose you'd call him. Frank drives the truck and does odd jobs around the place. There's grandma, and Walter, her husband. And Ward is there unless he's in town. A few children. And David."

"Who's David?"

Dabney giggled. "David is our buck negro. Every spiritual organization ought to have one."

"Huh. And what do you think will happen if we drive straight in on the main road?"

"I imagine everybody will come outside and stare at us, and if you behave in a threatening manner, they'll do their best to kill you."

"Maybe we'll send you in on your own."

Dabney made a choking sound. "I'm not welcome at Harmony Hamlet anymore! Don't make me go alone! Oh, dammit! Why do you want to go up there, anyway?"

Ray craned his neck round, briefly catching the eye of the cowering man in the back seat. "Hey, Clifford. Muriel is up there. We've got to go bring her home."

"Who's Muriel?"

"You know Muriel. My secretary. She types for you sometimes."

"Which one is she, the blonde girl?"

"Her hair's red."

"Oh, the girl with the funny nose. Muriel. What on earth is she doing all the way out there?"

"Looking for answers because you had to play dumb, you great idiot."

Anna wasn't chatty on the drive out to Harmony Hamlet, and Muriel didn't push her. The road was rough and winding in spots, and she focused on her driving. The cool shade of oaks was pleasant. It felt like any drive in the country, with an unknown destination up ahead. Muriel wondered if she'd be a different person when she came back down the hill. Out across the valley, she heard a steer bellow.

The road grew steep and shadeless, and after a bit Anna told her to stop and to honk four times, with a pause between. As Muriel complied, Anna rolled down the passenger window and whipped a green handkerchief back and forth. From higher up, a bright bell rang four times in response.

"You're all right now, they know we're coming."

Muriel crept up the narrow drive. On either side, deep gullies thick with vegetation ran down into the valley. The old trees were nearly strangled with vines. Prickly pods of wild cucumber hung down, glinting yellow-green and packed with fat seeds where the sun caught them. She thought she saw an old rusty automobile trapped against one of the trees. The first structures appeared, crummy little white-washed shacks built up close to the road, with rickety steps and narrow canvas porches.

Muriel felt eyes on her, but saw no one. A skinny red chicken darted in front of the car and she stomped on the brakes, veering a little too close to the drop. Anna laughed. "We don't bite, girl. And anyway, it's just a little farther to Mother's house." The car started with a shudder and they continued on up the hill.

More shacks. Stacks of wooden apple crates between them. A goat tethered to a porch pole, calmly gnawing a boot in the dust. Two little seated girls playing pat-a-cake. An unfinished mural of the musical angel on the front of a building, its long robe trailing off towards the dirt. Up on a cookhouse beam, a dinner bell swung in the breeze. Then at the crest, a glimpse of glass glinting through the trees. The road curved towards it, and widened, passed a big house and then ended against a rise. The green truck was already parked there. Muriel pulled up alongside it and stepped out into the late afternoon light.

Mother's house was a white and yellow two-story Cape Cod with projecting bay windows with arched eyebrows above. Lace curtains brushed the sills. Its apparent normalcy was broken by odd single-story stucco projections that rushed away on either side, deep blue with golden stars awkwardly applied. These structures were confusing, and a bit repellant. Muriel looked back to the house, and the white windowed door at its center.

Anna went up the steps, pried a key from a chatelaine at her waist, and opened the door. It was an ordinary wide entry with a whitewashed wooden bench opposite the staircase, a hall leading to the back of the house, and rooms, their stained pocket doors pulled shut, to either side. Anna told her to be seated and patient, and that Ruth would be

141

down to see her soon. Then she disappeared down the hall with no sound but the woosh of a heavy swinging door.

The bench was hard, the seat a little too low. Muriel tried not to look at her knees, which she thought were too bony. Scanning the room for distraction, she discovered a magazine rack flush against the bench. The only thing in it was a religious tract with the familiar angelic figure on the cover. She skimmed it, unable to focus on the strange text, then started when it fell open to a central page marked with a $100 gold certificate. She shut the tract and put it back where she'd found it.

She realized that her heart was beating hard. She closed her eyes and concentrated on sitting very, very straight with no expression on her face. "I am a tall tree," she told herself. "The wind doesn't move me. I am a rod of iron."

She sat and waited at the door of the house of secrets. Somewhere at the back of the hall, she thought she heard whispering. Or maybe it was just the blood in her ears. Outside, dusk was falling.

Down in the valley, Tom told Ray to pull over and he took the wheel. They drove on in silence. Outside Chatsworth, Tom left the road and stopped at a diner. "You two go in," Tom directed. "Get some more coffee in him."

He drove on into town and went to the Sheriff's office. It was in an old schoolhouse, a single room with a storage loft above. All the windows were open and a skinny old fellow was deep in his chair, feet kicked up on the desk, snoring. Tom rapped on the door jamb. The man woke languidly. He stretched, lowered his legs, tilted his hat back and made cool eye contact. He grinned.

"You're a long way from home, Tom James. Somebody rustle a Hollywood cowboy's pony?"

"Hey, Lew. I'm looking for a missing girl. Hoped you could give me a hand."

"Kidnap?"

"I hope not. Busybody. She's been poking around a religious group, some place up in the hills near here."

"Ah, hell, not the Great Eleven?"

"Yeah. You know them?"

"Hard not to. Half the valley wants them run out of the county, other half sneaks up onto the ridge line to watch them dancing."

"Dancing."

"Naked dancing." A chuckle, and a head shake. "Sure, I'll go up with you. Nothing else doing today." He got up, pulled his coat on, and strapped a holster round his waist. Sewn to his coat was an etched silver badge about as big around as a saucer. "She pretty?"

"Not too, but she's nice." Tom filled him in on Muriel, Ray, the Dabneys and the job at hand.

Twenty minutes later, Lew Wells was driving a few car lengths behind Tom on the road back to the diner. He parked out of sight behind a stand of eucalyptus. Tom went in alone. Dabney and Ray were in a booth in the back. They both had nearly full plates, Ray's a chicken dinner with mashed potatoes, Dabney's a hamburger sandwich. There was a coffee pot on the table.

Tom slid in next to Ray and told Dabney to beat it. Dabney looked befuddled and didn't move, so Tom spelled it out for him. "The big boys need to talk, Clifford. You go back to the bathroom, and wash your hands until the count of five hundred. Go on now." Dabney cast a sad look at his dinner, stood and shuffled to the back of the building. He stepped inside the door marked with a silhouette of a handlebar mustache.

"Do you have to be so hard on him? He's broken already."

"That's all the more reason to keep up the pressure. His sort, you let up and he'll do almost anything to prove he's really a man. Don't forget that, Ray, or you'll have cause to regret it."

"I suppose. But he's just so pathetic."

"He is that. But the fact is, I need to update you on the plan, without Old Man Trouble getting wise."

"The plan's changed?"

"It has. You and Dabney will go up to Harmony Hamlet alone and see Mrs. May Blackburn. Find out if Dabney can't get her talking about where his money's gone. She'll either talk or she won't, so don't waste too much time if it seems like a dry hole. Do get a sense of the layout up there. If you happen see Muriel, don't let her out of your sight, but don't go looking for her. Got that?"

"I've got it. What about you?"

"I'll be coming in with a constable friend who knows the area. He's a tough guy, but we probably won't need that. We'll do what we can to make sure you get out all right, and we'll try to find Muriel and bring her out as well." He palmed his pocket watch. "Whatever happens, let's try to meet here again at 10 o'clock. If either one of us doesn't make it out, the other calls Sheriff Clark and tells him to send men in to bring them out. It won't wait until morning."

At the back of the room, the toilet door waggled, revealing Dabney's sallow cheek and one wild eye. Tom nodded, and Dabney returned to the table, head bowed. He nosed around his cold hamburger, then took a lonesome bite. His hands, wrapped around the bun, were chapped from cheap soap.

The waitress came and slid an oozing slab of cherry pie onto the table beside Dabney and cocked her hip against the

145

booth. "Here you go, hon. And tell me if it isn't the best you've had this summer." He brightened and half smiled. The waitress walked away.

Tom slid the plate over to his side of the table, snatched Dabney's fork and ate a third of the pie in one bite. "Nope, not bad. Okay, you two, get moving. You're going on alone."

Ray got out of the far side of the booth and put his hat on. Dabney didn't move. A sheen of sweat broke out on his top lip. He stared at Tom, then shook his head.

"B-b-b-ut aren't you coming with us? I can't go up there just with him. You don't understand. Mother is very, very angry with me."

"I'm sure she has every reason to be angry with you, Clifford. That's why you're going to go and visit and make up with her. Ray can handle it. You can handle it. The two of you will go up to Harmony Hamlet, and you will talk to Mother. If I thought it was too dangerous, I wouldn't be sending you. Now get out of here. I've wasted enough time on your stupid troubles." He bent over the pie plate, then looked up at Clifford with narrowed eyes. The rich man's nephew shuddered, stood and skittered into the parking lot.

Tom smiled up at Ray, his eyes warm now. "I am truly sorry there's no time for you to have some of this fine, fine pie. Pay the bill on your way out, will ya? We won't be but fifteen minutes behind."

Ray turned, then paused. "How tough is this friend of yours, anyway?"

"How tough is Lew?" Tom shook his head and chuckled. "Oh, Lew Wells is something else. Sit down. Let me tell you one Lew story. There were some bums monopolizing the benches out in front of the Moorpark station, and bothering the ladies when they'd come into town. Station master tries to run 'em off, no luck. Couple guys from the store across the road try talking with them, even offering them a little cash to blow, but that doesn't work either. So then they call up Lew. Tell him what's what. He says, 'Leave those so-and-sos alone, I'll take care of them.' Okay. He shows up on Sunday morning with a couple of gas bombs and a mask to match. Rolls the grenades right up under the benches. The bums scatter, choking and sick. The whole town's watching. But Lew's not done yet. He charges in, chops one of the benches up with a hand-axe and tossed the pieces in the road. Scared the hell out of those fellows, and they haven't showed themselves back in Moorpark since."

"That's tough all right," allowed Ray.

"Well, this isn't Los Angeles. The law does things differently in the country."

"That's so. I hope we won't need your friend, all the same. But I guess I'm glad we have him."

147

Thirteen

Then, finally, after she'd been sitting long enough to feel strange and stiff, Muriel heard something stir at the top of the stairs. She looked up, then rose to her feet in mindless tribute.

A beautiful girl was at the top of the landing. Her hair was brown with hints of red and curled down around her cheeks in natural waves. She was dressed in a thick white robe belted with a golden rope. Her brown sandaled toes poked out. Her hands and elbows were pressed together in a mannered, sculptural pose. Her hips canted in an eloquent contrapposto. She came forward down the steps, smiling, and Muriel felt clean and bright, like a child who had been forgiven.

"Welcome, dear Muriel! I am Sister Ruth. We are so glad you've come! It is so fine to see you!" And she opened her arms as if to embrace the world.

So this was the daughter! She understood how Dabney might have given all his money away, and why ordinary old ladies were willing to ruin their hands sorting walnuts and live in drafty shacks in the mountains. None of that mattered as long as this beautiful girl would turn her wide face towards you and smile, even if just once in a while.

Or she could imagine feeling that way, while another part of her mind stood outside and watched all that was happening, Muriel playing the unworthy supplicant, Ruth the exalted priestess, and unknown others lurking in their hiding places upon the hill or closer still. The two women stepped through the smoothly-sliding pocket doors to the west, and once inside, Ruth pulled them shut again, locking the pair in instant intimacy.

It was a sitting room, lamp-lit and cozy. Ruth gestured to a dove-grey velvet couch. It was wide and soft, and smelled of rosewater. Ruth settled into a deep matching armchair opposite, legs tucked up beneath her.

The pretty girl was too perfectly framed by the pretty room. Long lilac curtains hung behind her from a slim iron bar. There were good paintings of California scenes, bright Chinese rugs, a pair of tall Rookwood vases on the mantle, and just beside Ruth, a black bird cage on a pole, scrupulously clean, in which a bright green parrot with red spots on its cheeks hung upside-down.

149

The bird knew his part, too: he gazed lovingly at the priestess and chuckled.

Very well, it was a stage set. Muriel folded her hands in her lap and waited for the show to begin.

Anna returned, now wearing a maid's costume, with a lace cap that was sillier than what she'd had on before. She set a wooden tray down on the table between the women, tea in a silver pot, flowered porcelain cups on matching saucers, thin slices of frosted white cake, lemon wedges, sugar cubes, and a single cornflower in a tall silver bud vase. She curtsied. Ruth dismissed her with a bored wave from graceful fingers. Then she reached over and poured their tea.

"I have heard such nice things about you, Miss Muriel."

How was it that she'd planned to play it? She'd thought about acting dumb—just a stray nut sorter with stars in her eyes—but now that she was actually in the room with Ruth, their conversation seemed to write itself. She felt suddenly sarcastic, and she didn't care who knew it.

"Have you? How sweet. And what nice things have you possibly heard? About how neatly I stack the walnuts?"

Ruth laughed. "No, silly. That you have lovely manners, quick hands and a generous spirit."

"And that I have a new car."

Ruth's eyes flashed. She wasn't used to being sassed. But, like Muriel, she let the wind steer her sails, and laughed again.

"Oh, do you?"

"Mmm-hmmm. It's a burgundy Hupmobile, and it's just outside."

"Well, maybe you'll take me for a spin some time. We've got some wonderful roads around Harmony Hamlet. Very exciting driving. But I truly was told that you have a generous spirit, and that quality interests me."

"Oh, it was only candy. Your friends shared with me first."

"That's what we do in Harmony Hamlet, Muriel. We share."

"How do you mean?"

"We share everything. Food and shelter, of course, but it's the more profound gifts that we are most pleased to exchange."

"Like which for instance?"

"Oh, good fellowship, family feeling, knowledge. A sense of belonging somewhere—of going somewhere."

The two women stared at each other across the stillness of the room, both of them needing something, but neither ready to ask for it outright.

"They are all beautiful ideals, but I don't see where I fit in. How exactly can I help you, Miss Ruth?"

"As a matter of fact, I thought that I might be able to help you."

151

"By inviting me to join your club?"

"No, not exactly. I wanted to offer you a job."

"A job? What kind of a job?"

Ruth cast her palms out, as if smoothing a map. "Sort of an advance girl, in real estate. I'd need you to visit a few places, make some observations, talk to some people, then come back and tell me just every little thing. The pay will be good, and your expenses will be covered, and there's nothing unpleasant in the job. Does that sound like something you could do?"

"Anyone could, I guess. But why me in particular?"

"Well, the fact is that we got a message from God that someone was coming—someone special, in a shiny red car. That someone is you, my dear. And we've got just the place ready for you—assuming you're ready for us."

The priestess stood up and made a small bow, which set her curls springing. "There's something outside that I must attend to. Why don't you just sit for a bit and think about it? You may have some questions, and I'll be happy to answer them, in a little while."

"All right. I'll think about it, and I will certainly have some questions."

"I'll see you again soon. And once we've talked it over, I hope you'll stay with us for dinner. Or even stay the night if you like. There's a pleasant guest room if you want it. And the drive down the mountain isn't so nice after dark."

"No, I guess it isn't. Thank you, Ruth."

"Don't thank me, silly. Thank God."

Fourteen

They'd been on the road again for just a few minutes when Dabney blurted out an urgent demand that Ray stop the car. As the wheels slowed on the gravel, Dabney tore his door open and ran to a ditch, where he crouched and emptied his stomach.

Ray remembered Tom's instructions and fought back the impulse to be kind. It was easier than he expected.

He sat at the wheel staring straight ahead, remembering a time as a boy when he had been so upset about an exam that he had vomited in an umbrella stand, and how the other boys had mocked him, and one big boy who he'd particularly admircd had unfurled the filthy umbrella towards him, coating him in a stinking shower of shame.

A wave of sympathetic nausea came on, then passed.

He didn't recall what had happened next. Something nasty to do with the showers. He didn't want to think about it anymore. It was a long, long time ago in a very different world than this one.

He waited, not patiently, for the sick man to collect himself. They had work to do. He wanted this day to be done, Muriel to be sitting alongside him, and with no particular place to go. He wanted a drink. He badly wanted to talk to Warren Lloyd one more time, one of their wonderful half-day talks about their dreams and obligations and the compromises that came between. He wanted to tell Joseph Dabney to his jowly old face that he was a bully and a fool and that the only reason anyone listened to him was that he was, by some incomprehensible quirk, still rich even after Julian fleeced him, but that one day he would be food for worms. He wanted to drive away and leave Clifford Dabney with his pool of sick and the wrong shoes for walking. He wanted to want to kiss his wife. He wanted to start again.

Dabney got back in the car, sourness surrounding him. The knees of his expensive linen trousers were stained. He stared out the window. The road opened up before them and they went on towards Harmony Hamlet, for want of any other destination.

The shadows lengthened. When it was time, Dabney gave directions. Ray obeyed with tight, formal motions. The big car took the grade with ease. A feeling of weird anticipation enrobed them both. Ray felt Dabney's fear and was excited by it. Anything could happen. And after it did, they would be mercifully free of each other.

"Stop here."

Ray did. The engine growled. They were on the out-skirts of a little settlement. He saw smoke above a roofline, and a flash of movement in the trees. Dabney was poking around in his trouser and jacket pockets. He opened the glove box and rooted there. He whipped around and looked in the back seat. Then he looked at Ray, shook his head and blurted something nonsensical.

"Oh, what's the matter now?"

"Do. You. Have. A. Green. Handkerchief?"

"What? No, of course not. My handkerchief is white. Here, do you need it?"

"Damn. Damn it. No, no, wait." Dabney fished a bank-note out of his wallet, and commenced fluttering it outside his window with wide swinging motions. "I think, yes, this is fine. Now, honk the horn, bap-bap-bap-bap, four times quick like that, then wait, then bap-bap-bap-bap again."

Ray honked the horn.

There was a long silent moment. They both sat staring straight ahead as the horn's echoes faded, and then, from above, a high, keening bell rang the same rhythm, dang-dang-dang-dang...bongggggggg...dang-dang-dang-dang.

Dabney let his breath out, and without thinking, mopped his forehead with the money.

"Go on. Drive. We are welcome."

Ray engaged the gears and resumed his crawl up the hill. They passed little cottages with no sign of life. The place was a dump, all dirty walls and cheap construction. At a curve, a stocky older woman with sagging features and a heavy wool wrap was suddenly standing before them. She lifted her arms and stared bullets at Dabney through the windshield. Ray stopped the car.

Dabney breathed hard. "Mother."

Ray looked at the old woman and tried to see some rough magic in her, something that could so frighten the man at his side that he swore he could hear his teeth chatter. But it wasn't there.

Dabney opened his door and moved towards the woman, clinging to the hood like a blind man. Her hard gaze didn't waver.

Ray remembered something Warren Lloyd once told him about watching out for people who didn't blink enough, and not trusting them with anything you cared about. Dabney, meanwhile, had reached the woman. She hissed something, turned on her heel and stomped into an open cookhouse beside the road. Dabney followed meekly, and a moment later, so did Ray.

Up close, May Blackburn was imposing. Her body was solid; muscular without fatness. Her chin was firm, with a delicate cleft. She had a wide, down-turned mouth, a slightly piggish nose and large dark eyes framed by thick brows. She sat with authority on the short bench at the head of the cookhouse table, with big hands laid flat before her. He could recognize something of the successful businessman in her manner. The world would come to her if she only waited.

Dabney was still standing as Ray approached. Some unspoken message passed between them, and Dabney relaxed, then straddled the long bench beside the table. She gazed up at Ray, and made a bored gesture to the space opposite Dabney. He sat, and she turned the full force of her attention onto her errant devotee.

Her voice was her secret.

Ray didn't think he'd ever heard a one like it. The sound was so musical, so ripe with erotic energy, that a good ten seconds elapsed before he recognized the sounds she was making as words, and began to process them.

They were words, all right, though not words he'd ever heard from a woman's mouth. May Blackburn was systematically eviscerating Clifford Dabney with all the skill of a butcher trimming fat. Her brutal precision made old man Dabney's rages seem like the tantrums of a schoolgirl. And as she cursed the man, questioning his intelligence, his virility and his value to the species, Dabney stared at her with a mix of love and awe that was hideous to behold.

"So here you are, again, you little worm. Crawling back to your Mother to suck at her teats. A stupid man, a vain man, a little tiny man who is hardly a man at all. Dragging your filthy, clammy flesh, a naked slug underneath expensive fabrics that only make you look and smell nastier to everyone here. Why have you come back, Clifford? Because we do not want you!"

Dabney shot a look at Ray, as if seeking strength from his companion. But the disgusted expression on the other man's face just sucked the last of his self away. He knew there was something he was supposed to say, some questions he had agreed to ask, but all he could think of was Mother's thick mouth, curling over sharp little teeth, saying the things that he had always thought about himself, the things that were so different from everything else Mother had said to him over the past five years.

His ingrained manners came to the fore, in spite of everything. "I-I'd like to introduce you to Ray Chandler," he managed. "Mr. Chandler and I work together at the oil company. Mr. Chandler, may I present Mrs. May Blackburn? She is a—she is a prophetess." The final, stuttered words rose upward in a question that was not a question.

Dabney looked down at his hands, which were trembling.

When he first came, she was so kind to him. He had never felt more at home with another person—not his own mother, not his wife. He yearned to be near her—to learn what she knew—to merely soak up the peace that seemed to flow out of her body and fill every room she inhabited with warm, calm air.

And she liked him, too—he knew she did. She said she saw the divine in his movements, and told him how he could be more holy in his everyday actions, even when eating, breathing and excreting. She gave him a sacred name and the spiritual practice which instilled his name with the power of life and death.

At her direction, he purchased the four beautiful animals, each of a different color, required for the Concord of the Horses' Hoof and the Breathing In. And later, he personally poured the steaming water over their backs and felt pure and fresh while the creatures, who were only symbols, pawed the earth and screamed.

After years of seeking, of visits to mediums and yogis, of a mass in the Vatican celebrated mere hours after he had writhed naked in the blood of a bull inside a backstreet Mithraeum, his senses flooded but unmoved by fiercely shouting Pentecostal preachers and the soft song of the Quaker Friends, always looking for the thing which he felt himself

160

lacking, he had discovered it in the face of an old Oregon woman, and the weird and faithful group she had collected around herself.

With Mother's love, he had felt himself emboldened to be the greatest possible Clifford Dabney, a being of fiery light and harsh justice. A Master. A Man.

And while he had basked in the unfamiliar feelings of power and purity, he knew now that she had reared back her abdomen and plunged a powerful stinger into the very heart of his inherited wealth, draining the money, the oil leases, the rental checks, even his wife's dowry away.

She had somehow known exactly how much there was inside of him, and as the bottom was scraped, she'd suddenly jettisoned him from her heart and cast him back out into the harsh, real world.

It had happened so decisively that he'd scarcely understood it at the time. One evening he was the Hereafter and Now, at the center of the Great Circle, entrusted to wash and oil the women before the coming Moon Dance. The next morning before dawn he was pulled roughly from the holy feather bed in which he lay with Ruth beside him, then shoved into the back of the green panel truck with a rough sack over his head, tied too tightly with rope around his midsection. He fell on top of a figure that grunted and then retched, and when he reached out to free himself with clawlike hands bound to his hips, he found his wife's naked ass.

She was sobbing under her sack, and he rolled away from her in disgust. The truck's engine turned over and the driver gunned it recklessly down the mountain road. The prisoners in the back were bruised and scratched. Ejected from Eden. Wretched and alone, together.

They could speak through their hoods, but there was nothing to say. In time, they fell into something like sleep, only to start awake in fear as the back doors were thrown open and rough hands grabbed and pulled them down onto a flat, paved road. They couldn't see anything. There were two men. Dabney thought they might be Ward and Frank Rizzio, but neither one had ever laid hands on him before, and had certainly never grasped his testicles and pulled him, like an animal, up a driveway, across a wet lawn, up a few steps and into the entryway of what proved to be his own home, where he was shoved to the rug, the rope around his middle slashed with a strong pull of a blade, and left gasping for breath beside his humiliated bride.

He'd pulled the bag off his head and blinked against the light. The door of his house gaped open. He saw David, the Negro, sitting in the passenger seat of the truck as it slowly pulled away. He dropped shamed to his knees and vomited on the threshold.

Behind him he was aware that Alice was crying, but didn't care. He knew only his own humiliation, compounded when he raised his head and saw the open-mouthed newsboy at the end of the walk, leather satchel clutched to his heart. The boy ran away. Dabney got up, stepped into his home, and closed the door.

How was it he'd forgotten his humiliation until this moment, facing Mother again? It had been in the back of his mind like a bit of food stuck in a tooth, yet when it loomed up at him he had pretended that it was just something ugly that he'd dreamed.

He and Alice had not spoken of it. She went to her room, he to his, where they had washed themselves and dressed as if it were an ordinary day. There was no newspaper, but he'd read yesterday's in the garden. Around 3, he'd gone into the office, where he fell asleep in his armchair, soothed by the scent of leather and the ticking of the wall clock. His uncle asked him to dinner, and he phoned Alice and told her to be ready at 7.

Everything was normal, was super normal, except the growing realization that he was almost without funds. After a few days, he manufactured a narrative and tried it out on his uncle. The old man seemed to see through his story, but also to feel a little sorry for him. He said that everything would be all right if he would only sit back and let the grown-ups take care of things. They had played these parts before. Chandler was put on the case, and Dabney locked Alice up and checked himself in for a rest cure.

It was only then that he allowed himself to collapse. He got very drunk in the parking lot of El Encanto, and when a groundsman found him and took him to Dr. Cravens he told the doctor some small bit of what had happened to him. Even drunk, he couldn't bring himself to talk about David's hands on his body.

The doctor said he had had a shock and that his psyche needed an opportunity to reknit itself where it had been ripped open. He prescribed injections, massage and hot soaks. Dabney floated in a dream land. He felt fine, he really did. And then he was again cast out of Eden, picked up by his uncle's toady Ray and that odious Tom James and forced to face the new, cruel Mother.

He wasn't ready.

He started to cry.

He looked at Ray, and shrugged hopelessly, palm extended across the table in a plea for help. Ray turned away, shaking his head with small, convulsive tremors. Dabney gulped in air and wiped his eyes with his sleeve, looked back at Mother and blurted "So-what-did-you-do-with-all-my-money-huh?"

For a long moment, the broken man and the old woman just stared across the table. Then her right hand shot out, like a bolt from a gun. She caught Dabney's lower lip in her fingers and twisted it cruelly. His face seemed to collapse around her claw, a flower nectar-moist at the center.

A little blood dripped onto the table top. She reeled him in towards her, his body rising in his seat to avoid literal mayhem. With no seeming effort, she pulled him very, very close. When his nose was inches from hers and his twisted lips dripping with gore and spit and snot, she suddenly released her grasp and let his unbalanced figure crash onto the table.

"You little fool," she hissed. "Any money in your care would be better in the sewer. How dare you inquire what form your tributes took after they left your hands?"

She turned to Ray and smiled indulgently. Then, in that lovely, throbbing voice, she began to tell him a story.

"Do you know what Clifford wanted more than anything else? He spoke of this often when he lived with me. Why, this little man desired to gain power over life and death. Oh, imagine it! Like Jesus himself, to roll away the stone and reveal still flesh made quick again. But Clifford sought not to reverse unjust passage or reunite heartbroken families with their loved ones, oh no. He wanted to kill for pleasure, then bring his victims back and kill them again! Isn't that right, Clifford?"

The man slumped against the table, his head pinioned on a triangle of his elbows and fingers. He shook his head slowly and whimpered, and dabbed at his lip with the back of his hand. May went on, relentless.

"This was his fantasy: he would drive down Broadway on the back of a monstrous machine, half thresher, half calliope. Hypnotic music would draw them out of the shops and the streetcars, deliver them up like little lambs come on their own to the killing floor. Poisonous steam would pour out of the chimney, dazing them where they stood. Up in the saddle rode our great hero, leering down on important businessmen and on babes in arms, on beautiful women, cowboys, street singers, hobos and whores, writers and architects, bankers and bakers, the wretched and the fortunate, the citizens of this young city, all of them in his thrall and at his mercy.

"Oh, I wish that you could have seen it! Clifford would become so excited when he imagined all of them, standing before his terrible metal beast, unable to break away and run. Then, in his imaginings, he would throw the gears and drive on—backward and forward—expertly mowing down everyone who stood before him, in an orgy of knives and fear. You would realize how very funny this is, if you have ever been unfortunate enough to be a passenger in an automobile that Clifford was driving! But every man is a genius in his own daydreams. Is that not so, Mr. Chandler?"

She didn't wait for an answer, but powered on.

"And every one of the slaughtered bodies would somehow be intact when he was done, bearing no sign of the cutting blade's impact, simply D-E-A-D. And he'd look back in gladness at all the souls brought down by his impulse. And of course among them was his great tormentor, amidst all the anonymous strangers who would fall before his wheel, Uncle Joseph, with his smirk, and his millions of dollars and his grotesque little pot belly dangling over stripy trousers. Isn't that right, Clifford? Your great uncle would be just one of the crowd, mowed down with all the rest and tossed into a pile like a piece of cordwood.

"Oh! And do you know what else? Clifford was going to build a tall and beautiful building on the edge of town, its walls massive pipes pumped through with icy waters. And he was going to transport all the people he had killed to this building, shovel them into elevators and take them to the cooling floor. And when he felt like doing it all again, he'd bring his victims back to life and let them wake up all piled together like scraps of wool, confused and frightened. These dazed dreamers would find their ways out of the building and back to Broadway, and when they did, Clifford would simply kill them all again.

"Well, I suppose that was a pretty daydream for a little man who wished that he was big. Don't you think so, Mr. Chandler?"

This time she paused and waited for his answer.

"Ahem. I imagine, Mrs. Blackburn, that almost anyone can be encouraged to embroider an unpleasant fantasy in the proper circumstances. Every man has doubts about himself, and sometimes imagines that he is more powerful than he actually is. Maybe not a god, but something more powerful. I don't like to judge another's man's daydreams, Mrs. Blackburn. I would not wish for mine to be published."

Bang-bang-bang! Dabney pounded his fists on the table, careless as he smeared his own blood droplets. "O Mother! Please just tell him where the money is, so I can go away again! Oh, please do!"

"Money, Clifford? What money is that?"

Her smile was a shark's, her voice richly sarcastic. Or was she the jaguar, straddling a tree branch above the water hole, waiting for some careless creature to stop and drink before dying? Ray felt frightened for Dabney. He was poised at the moment before the chasm. She had been just toying with him until now.

"The money I gave you. The oil leases. The rentals. The money. My—you know what money!"

She turned her gaze full on him, and he flinched.

"I wonder how you dare to bring an infidel to my sanctuary and speak of such filthy things? Money? Money is of the world and the city. I live with God, and the angels talk to me. Oh, you speak of money? Show your belly, little pig! Roll on your back and wiggle your piggy hips! Money-money-money! Wiggle-wiggle-wiggle! That's right, Clifford!

Very good! Wiggle, piggy, wiggle! Now make your piggy sounds."

It was finally enough for Ray. He put his hand on her wrist and spoke very firmly. "Stop it, Mrs. Blackburn. You've said enough now. Just leave him be. God. You bitch."

She gasped and pulled her arm away, stood quickly and stepped a few steps back. For a moment, Ray thought he'd frightened her. But her expression was weird, serene.

Then he heard the low growl. He turned to see Dabney glaring at him, lips thin and white. He remembered Tom's warning that he should not be kind to Dabney.

This was absurd. He'd had his fill. He stood up and turned back towards the car.

Dabney brought him down before he left the cookhouse, with an unsporting elbow jab to the kidneys. They rolled into the dirt, neither one quite gaining an advantage.

Dabney was weak from the drugs and indolence. Ray was no fighter, but he wouldn't be beaten. He wanted to get up and away from the younger man, who disgusted him. But he didn't dare badly harm his employer's kin. If he could neutralize Dabney, then get the car, he could take him away from here.

He flashed suddenly on one fight in the dormitory when he was a day student at Dulwich. How did that little Welsh boy pin the big bully, Asquith? Something with the legs

169

wasn't it? Yes, inflicting pain there at the top of the thigh and then pushing hard when his opponent wavered. Yes, yes—he was getting the better of Dabney, who seemed so weak and small under his body. He felt a disquieting urge to humiliate the other man, to strip or shear him. Instead, he pushed up and away, silently entreating the other man to stay down, to let it be ended before it got too ugly.

On a ridge not far away, Lew squinted down through the sight of his rifle, and said "Much more of this, and we'd better go on in."

"Yeah. I guess Dabney's crazier than I thought."

"Everyone's crazy in Harmony Hamlet. You'll be, too, if you hang around."

Fifteen

Muriel sat where Ruth had left her, ankles crossed, handbag at her side, chin cocked. Her eyes scanned the room slowly, her ears tracking, too. It seemed inconceivable in this place, but she thought she might truly be alone. If she was being watched, she couldn't feel it.

She might wait for Ruth's return, stay for supper and perhaps the night, learning little enough, or she could delve deeper into the weird house now, searching for what she'd come to find.

She wasn't frightened. She was curious. She knew she could be quick. She decided.

She made a circuit of the room, opening the cupboards. All were empty but for dust. She looked behind the curtains and found a solid wall. The parrot chuckled softly. Nothing in this theatrical room had any use beyond providing Ruth with a backdrop for her beauty. Now that the young priestess was gone, the paintings seemed trite and the perfume in the air cheap and a little poisonous.

She went into the hall and tried the door opposite. It was locked. She knelt and put her eye to the keyhole, but the room beyond was dark. Turning back to the front door, she noticed a key hanging from a brown ribbon on a hook. Funny that she hadn't seen it before. The key fit the lock. Inside she found another sitting room, laid out precisely like the one in which Ruth had received her.

But everything about this room was more masculine. Here the perfume was lavender with undertones of civet. The furniture was heavy wood upholstered in dark stained leather, the rug crimson with a black border. Brown velvet curtains hung behind a throne-like armchair. Beside it, a painting of a ship tossed on a storming sea, and tall hammered brass vases, formerly shell casings, framed the mantle. Here, too, all of the cupboards were empty.

She locked the door again and started up the staircase where Ruth had made her dramatic entrance. It went up to a landing, then swung around one half turn. She took the steps quickly, fingers light on the banister.

Just past the landing she stopped, suddenly confused.

There was no second story to the building.

Instead of opening, as it logically must, onto a hallway with rooms all along it, the staircase went right up to a flat ceiling. The wall was on her left hand, open banister on her right. The ceiling had a hatch in it, and a small brass handle. She pushed up. Nothing happened. She slid the handle to the left. The panel opened out, and she took the steps all the way up to the broad, flat roof of the strange house.

It was near dark now. Down below on the hillside she thought she heard raised voices. But a false front on the house was too tall to see over. There was nothing to stand on. The stony hill was flush against her back. It felt claustrophobic and strange, like a carnival fun house. She half expected the ground to suddenly spin and send her flying. She saw a second panel in the floor, some small distance from the first. She lifted it, revealing another staircase, this one narrow and walled on both sides. She took it down into the kitchen at the back of the house.

The kitchen was a windowless square equipped with an eight-burner stove, walk-in icebox, deep larder and large copper pots hanging from hooks on the ceiling beams. A tall coconut cake sweated under a glass dome on the counter. The only door, next to the staircase, led into the hall and back out to the twin sitting rooms. There was a tiny water closet just opposite this door, and nothing else to the house.

Muriel felt dizzy from the trip up the trick staircase. What was this place? There wasn't anything to see.

What was she missing? What about the windowless side wings? Was there some way to enter them from in the house?

She wheeled around, throwing open cupboards. There was no mystery here. It was an ordinary kitchen, stocked for baking. Bread dough was proofing under damp rags in the oven. Silverware soaked in a soapy solution in the sink. The larder had a small deer hung by its leg from a big hook, cheeses on shelves, buckets of milk with plates on top. The icebox was neat as a pin, stocked with only eggs and butter.

She turned back to the larder. Was something strange about its dimensions? She ran her fingers over the narrow shelves. Her fingers found a button. She fiddled with it. A cracking noise, and the wall before her suddenly gaped. Behind it, a dark passage opened up. The air was cold and smelled of damp.

She picked up a small Vulcanite torch from the shelf and tested the light. It was strong. She wrapped the cord around her wrist, took one look back at the empty room, then stepped softly into the unknown.

Now she cast the light beam up and around. Rough hewn, glittering stone walls framed the passage, just tall enough for her to walk through without crouching. The path was about twenty feet wide, narrowing quickly to half that. It was soft sand over stone, with a slight downward angle.

Suddenly, she understood the weird layout of the house. It had been built to hug the hill, because it was a part of the hill. The structure continued deep inside the earth. This was the mouth of the mountain.

Dare she go further? The thrill of recognition answered a resounding yes. She set a dishrag down to keep the larder door from locking and turned her attention to the gaping hole ahead.

She had been in show caves before. This was not one of those clean, roped-off caverns meant to appeal to the genteel terror of tourists. These walls were irregular and ugly, set in here and there with deposits of gritty-looking crystals, some of which had been roughly harvested, leaving gaping holes. There were boxes of potatoes and carrots stored alongside the path, with stray loose vegetables a hazard beneath her feet. The floor was irregular, its incline sometimes pitching to one side then back to the median. The air smelled smoky, moist and a little rotten. It was colder than was comfortable.

But she didn't care about the cold. There must surely be some revelation within, some key to the mystery that she could absorb, then bring back to Los Angeles, set on Joseph Dabney's desk, and be the heroine of the hour. That recognition would make her weird adventure worth it, never mind the walnut stains and the sore neck, or the feelings of uncertainty that had flowed in like a new tide along with her solitude.

She would hurry, explore the cave, find its secrets, get out again and off this mountain before full darkness fell.

She passed the last of the vegetables. The path narrowed, veered left and ran straight on and slightly down. She rubbed her shoulders for warmth. Up ahead, something shone in the darkness. She whipped her torch around, then switched it off. The distant light flickered. She wondered if her eyes were tricking her. Continuing on, the cave grew so low that she had to bend her knees. She put her hands against the roof to steady herself.

Then the walls and ceiling opened up again, so wide that it was dizzying. Muriel swung her torch around, piecing the fragmented scene together in her mind. It wasn't like anything she'd ever seen. A low arch, brilliantly white, enclosed the giant room, set on a pitch that led down to six separate tunnels, set too regularly to be natural, against the stone. The floor was white sand. The walls were smooth and pale, with warped forms like inverted sandcastles jutting from the roof.

She spotted the odd light again. It was at the mouth of the rightmost tunnel below. Water was dripping, somewhere. She moved towards the light, falling twice on the soft, slanting sand. It didn't hurt. What was that scraping sound above—an animal? Rocks falling? She didn't hear it again.

To reach the lighted tunnel at the base of the steep, sandy slope, she had finally to lurch forward, arms out, and catch herself against the solid rock wall between two openings. Her palms stung on landing. Then she half-crawled along the slanting wall, supporting her weight on her arms and hip, until she reached the opening in which a dim light flickered. The path leveled out, and she lurched on tired legs into the tunnel.

The first thing she saw was the metal lantern, set on the ground in a ring of flat stones. A thin shade cast its light upward, making crazy shadows out of small projections on the walls. It wasn't bright, but her eyes, dilated from the blackness of the cave, took a moment to adjust. Her torch hung at her side as she blinked and panted in the stillness. A ledge came into view, midway up the wall opposite, a little more than an arm's length away. Something bulky laid across it. It was hard to make out. She took the lantern by the handle, buoyed it up, and then froze, unbelieving.

The thing on the ledge was human, horribly contorted and apparently mummified. The face, thin and tortured, was cast towards her, mouth gaping in its final fishy gasp. Long white hair was matted to the paper skin of the skull. The eyelids were open, the eyes themselves sunken and discolored. One bony hand clutched at its clavicle. The hips were cast towards her with knees drawn up and poking out

177

from under a rough off-white robe. The legs seemed impossibly long, terribly thin. There was a lightweight black silk slipper on the foot nearest her, the kind of shoe her grandmother wore around the house. The smell of decay was faint, but sickening.

Muriel stood, unable to look away. The pain and fear in the mummy's face were like a physical blow. Worse, she perceived personality in the awful artifact. She thought she could tell what type of woman this had been before whatever nasty circumstance had killed her and brought her deep into the earth to be laid out like some ancient offering.

She felt sad and confused and sure, suddenly, that her plan had been foolhardy, perhaps even fatal.

A sudden rustling movement inside the robe. Oh, god no—rats!

She wheeled away, dropping the lantern, a shriek escaping her lungs, and ran full on into a warm, wide body. Strong hands grabbed her, spun her 'round, covered her mouth. Garlicky breath hissed "Shut up!"

She struggled in the dark, kicking and twisting, but he was too big and had her by the waist and the jaw. She couldn't breathe. Her feet left the ground. She was so tired, so small. It was so dark here. Desperate and too panicked to even feel afraid, she slumped in his arms and braced herself for some new terror.

But all he did was turn her to face him, tenderly brush the hair from her face, and whisper, "Will you please be quiet, so I can help you?"

"O-Okay."

"Don't move. I need to find the lamp." He stepped away and she heard him rooting around near where she knew the body lay in awful ecstasy.

She found she'd lost her torch in the struggle. She felt around the sandy cave bottom with her foot. The metal tube rolled away. She crouched, snatched it up and threw the switch. Illuminated in the pale beam was the truck driver who she'd followed out to the valley on Friday.

He screwed up his eyes, held his palms out and shook his head. "Please don't run, miss. It gets worse."

"Worse than this?" She swung the light over the dead woman, whose monstrous screaming profile ran up the cavern walls and onto the roof, where it broke up into meaningless shadows. She shifted the light into a pool by their feet. The white sand reflected upward, casting a gentle glow.

"God help us, worse than this."

He had a nice face. She decided she'd trust him, at least a little bit. He knelt and picked up the lantern, brushed sand away from the wick and struck a match. The lamp sputtered and flared. He held it over the corpse and looked down into its ruined face. He set the lamp down by the mummy's head, took a white rosary from his pocket and wrapped the beads in its clawed right hand, tucking the cross inside.

"Oh, Frances. I wish I could do more than this for you." He turned his head. "Are you a Christian?"

"No, I'm—no, sorry."

"It doesn't matter. Her name was Frances Turner, and she made wonderful cakes. Her sister Mary had passed, and she always honored her memory. She was my friend, and I don't think I'll ever forgive myself for not being there in her time of need."

His hand moved to stroke the white hair, but stopped half an inch away.

"What's your name, miss?"

"Muriel."

"Mine is Frank. Muriel, listen. I think I can get you out of here. It's going to be rough going, but if you follow my instructions, and if we're lucky, we can get off this mountain without anyone stopping us. Can you be quick, and wait quietly where I tell you?"

"I—yes—no. Look, why are you helping me?"

"Because I can't stand to see this—" he gestured to Frances on her stone slab— "happen to anybody else. Because I've been selfish. Come on—we can talk later—let's move now."

He stepped out of the death tunnel and turned to the far side of the big cave, holding the lamp low to illuminate their steps. Slowly they crept along the tilted path. At each of five dark-mouthed openings along the wall, she held her breath and tried not to think about what could be worse than what she'd already seen and smelled. They reached the far wall and she saw that there were broad metal rings set at regular intervals leading back up the sandy slope. Using them for support, the pair climbed quickly up through the soft, shifting sands.

"I'm not sure I could have gotten out without these rings," she whispered.

"No, probably not. But even if you did, you'd find the larder door locked now."

"You—?"

"Of course not. Ruth locked you in. She left you in the spook house with temptation hiding in plain sight, and when you grabbed for it, she rejoiced."

"But why—"

"Shhhh, later. Come on, we're nearly there."

He led her into another passage, this one straight and level. It ran away from the sand dune and its horrible inhabitant, and as she got farther away Muriel felt her nausea fade.

Finally a set of narrow stone steps delivered them to a small iron door set flush against the rock. He fished a long key from a ring in his pocket and set it into the mouth of the lock. It clicked and he pushed at the door. Then the evening light and fresh air gushed in. And with them, the sound of angry voices, somewhere down below. They stood together, breathing hard, as their eyes came back into focus.

The brush was thick here, shielding the hidden door. Just to their left, one wing of the windowless extension came to an end. She saw that its back wall did not actually touch the hillside, but merely skirted it, with a narrow walkway behind. He took her wrist and pulled her through the bushes and along this path, where they turned sideways and sidled with arms at their sides.

Here was a door, child-sized and painted gold. It had a massive knob inscribed with arcane symbols, but no hole for a key. He knelt and made a few careful manipulations of the knob, pressing and pulling at it. Sweat dripped down his neck and darkened his collar. She smelled woodsmoke and pine. The angry voices seemed very far away. It was like a dream. Maybe she was dreaming. Should she reach out and touch the man? Maybe he'd turn into something different, something winged that could lift her up and away from this awful place.

A crack, and the knob moved in the door. He pushed, and the panel opened upward on a hinge. He crawled in, then stuck his hand out for her to follow.

She went awkwardly down on all fours, only to find the floor inside covered with piles of velvet rugs, so thick that she sunk up to her wrists.

It was pure pleasure after the cold fear of the cave, and without thinking of how it looked, she rolled onto her back and threw her arms out in delight, then kicked her legs until they were outside the swing of the little door. He let it down slowly, then flopped down beside her with a grunt. They rested.

Then she turned over and looked around. The long, curving room was dimly lit by bulbs set inside a recess between the wall and ceiling. The walls, at least fifteen feet tall, were heavily plastered. A gigantic furniture set nearly filled the hall. In the center of the room hulked a vast throne-like chair, the edges of its leather seat studded with brads the size of halved grapefruit, its four feet the paws of a lion. Beside it, a heavy floor lamp stood, topped with a rough-hewn, life-sized carving of a lion's head.

Down at the end of the room, a hulking day bed huddled near an overstuffed chair, its matching stool pushed close. Massive twin dressers lurked against the long walls, their tops draped in beaded fringed shawls big enough to wrap elephants. Every bit of exposed wood was gilded, but thick aggregations of metal clogged the surfaces, giving an effect that was more repellant than baronial.

"What is this place?"

"We call it the Lord's Room, and this is the Lord's Furniture Set. And before you ask, I can't possibly explain now. Get under the bed, right in the center where you can't be seen, and wait there. I'll be back very soon for you, I promise. All right?"

"All right."

"Do you see the dresser, against the front wall?"

"Yes?"

"When you hear four knocks, I want you to pull out the bottom two drawers entirely, and crawl into the back of the dresser. They're not too heavy. You'll be all right. I can't do this for you, just in case one of them comes in before I get back. There's another little door there, and I'll be on the other side, and I'll let you out. All right?"

"But what if someone does come in?"

"Just be quiet. They won't be looking for you, and nobody stays long in this room."

"All right. Then what?"

"Then we'll both need to be quick. I'll open the hatch, you come through, and jump into the back of my truck. It won't be far away. I'm going to drive you out of here, and I won't be stopped. Got it?"

"Yes. I'll wait for you under the bed. I don't understand why you're helping me. But thank you."

He briefly clasped her little hands in his rough brown ones, and crawled backwards out through the tiny door. Muriel buried her fists in the soft velvet pile between her open thighs, then rose and took her place underneath the giant's bed. It still seemed like a dream, but no longer such a bad one. The thought of being off the mountain was delicious. She grabbed hold of the crossbars above her head and hung there in the silence. She hoped Frank wouldn't be long.

He wasn't long. The knocks came soft, but clear. The drawers weren't too heavy, though she was surprised to find them so wobbly and poorly made, with paint slopped halfway over the bottoms, and loose knobs. She shoved the cheap panels aside. Climbing inside the dresser, she caught her dress on a nail, tearing it as she struggled to pull free. She heard the grinding of gears inside the trick door, the crack, and then the dusk poured in.

"Come on, let's go! Follow me!"

Frank rose from his crouch and took off down the hill at a jog. She saw the truck, waiting with the back doors ajar, maybe a hundred yards away, and ran toward it. A hurried movement off to the left caught her attention, and she turned her head.

It was Ward, mounted on a tall, dappled horse and wearing a long Chinese robe that fanned out over the beast's rump.

185

His mustaches were blown straight back, and his mouth open in a leer. He had a long stick held out in front of him, and murder in his eyes.

He wasn't looking at her or Frank or the waiting truck. He was galloping straight for Ray, who was out in the middle of the road with his back turned, palms out, pushing Dabney away.

Dabney saw Ward first, shrieked and scooted over the side of the road. Ray wheeled around and locked eyes with Muriel. For an instant, she thought he might move towards her. But then he registered Ward's approach, blanched, and he too scuttled off the road like a frightened crab.

Her last sight of him was just the top half of his face, peeping at her from over a mound of dirt. He saw Frank shoving her into the back of the truck and he turned his head away. Then he slid down the hill and away from the rampaging Mandarin.

Up on the ridge, Lew Wells had had enough. He let out a furious howl, shouldered his gun, and took off quick down the chaparral-specked hillside. Tom followed close behind.

"Stop right there, you crazy sons of bitches!" hollered Lew.

Ward snatched up his horse's reins and gazed in horror at the constable. The horse wheeled around in confusion, and Ward fell backwards off his mount. He was stunned for a moment, and when he came to he was whimpering. For Lew Wells' reputation was so fearsome in the Santa Susanna hills that even Mother's avenging angel could be made to cower by the mere presence of the man.

Wells stalked over to the fallen horseman, took the stick away from him and broke it. Tom helped Ray and Dabney back up on to level ground. Far below, the truck carrying Frank and Muriel reached the mountain road.

"Don't hurt me, Mister Wells," begged Ward, who was sitting up now, tangled in his dusty robes and rubbing his coccyx. "I was only playing."

"Be quiet, you little freak. Tom, was that the girl?"

Tom affirmed that it was.

"All right. You—" he pointed to Ray, "Get the car. We're done here."

Ray started back down the hill. May had slipped quietly away, and all the cottages were shut up tight. He brought the car up. Then they left the holy mountain, under the protection of the only person in the hills that even madmen feared.

The men were quiet on the drive back to Los Angeles.

Tom was thinking about how it was that true believers could steer so far from paths of righteousness, not seeing that they'd left safe and godly ground. He thought about the

Holy Rollers he'd known as a boy, the more modest beliefs that powered Allie in her good works, and how he'd put faith on the back shelf in order to do some of the things required of a policeman. He thought about the Four Horsemen of the Apocalypse, and how small and silly Ward had looked flat on his back with his robes askew. He thought about May Blackburn's voice, and felt excited. He was glad the car was so loud. It didn't seem so lonely.

Ray kept playing the scene with Muriel over in his head, stopping and restarting his actions against the backdrop of queasy shame and his scratched and aching body.

Had he been cowardly, or prudent? Did it matter? What difference would it have made if he'd run out in front of the rampaging horse and Ward's swinging pike? He could have been struck down, even killed. Or he might have been fast enough, and reached Muriel ahead of the threat. What then? Pull her away from the younger man? Hit him? Be himself struck down? Bleed onto the dirt as a meaningless show for a woman not his wife?

He wasn't a man of brute force. It was unfair of her to expect him to be faster than a horse, stronger than a muscular youth.

Surely Muriel must understand why he'd gone over the side of the road.

He tried to remember the expression on her face, but it slipped away like quicksilver. Was she was angry or frightened or disappointed in him? Who knew? He didn't even know if she had gone willingly into the back of the truck or if the driver had forced her. It mattered terribly, and he had no clue.

Let her be all right, he thought, loud and strong in the part of himself that sometimes made entreaties to forces he could neither name nor understand.

He wondered if Dabney had seen anything. No, even if he had, Dabney wouldn't care. And he didn't want to give the man anything to lord over him by asking.

Dabney, in the back seat, didn't seem to be thinking about much of anything. After hyperventilating for a few moments, he'd simply rolled over onto his back and put his feet up onto the door. Soon his even breaths were synchronized with the rhythm of the tires on the highway. They drove on through the night and after a while the electric lights of Los Angeles brightened the sky and blotted out the stars. It was quiet in Hollywood, and the traffic on Western Avenue moved smoothly.

They stopped in front of Dabney's house, and Ray went to shake the sleeper.

"I'm awake," Dabney said, clasping Ray's wrist. "And I've been thinking. You two come inside. We need to talk."

Dabney's house was hot and smelled of dust and spoiled fruit. He took them into the den, which was decorated in

189

the height of the Spanish Colonial style, an excrescence of cascading armorial embroidery, wrought iron and model galleons on nearly every flat surface. The house wasn't even Spanish, but that hadn't stopped the decorator. Reddish light raked through a mica-shaded lamp planted on a wide library table, illuminating a heavy brass writing set seemingly meant for penning Imperial edicts. Dabney tied back red velvet curtains and opened the windows. Tom and Ray sat on cold leather chairs. Outside, a cat howled.

Dabney poured three glasses of Scotch from a cut glass decanter, then topped them up with seltzer from a bottle wrapped in chain-mail. Then he crossed the room to slide the pocket doors shut.

"You needn't close those doors." Ray observed. "I put Alice in a hotel for safekeeping."

There was a pause.

"You did what?" Dabney's normally yellowish pallor darkened.

"It seemed prudent, in light of the threatening note your friends left on her pillow."

Dabney's jealous rage, if it had been rage, fizzled into typical distraction.

"Oh, did they? Of course they would. Good thinking, Chandler. I might just go stay in a hotel myself. This damned house is hot in the summer. And cold in winter. And musty all the time."

Tom cleared his throat. "It's late, and we've all had a long day. What do you have in mind, man?"

Dabney emitted a dry cackle.

"What do I have in mind? Well, Tom James, I'll tell you what I have in mind. Getting on with my life, how does that sound? Cleaning up the dog's mess. Saving my soul, I suppose. And apologizing, to both of you. Because, it wasn't supposed to be like this. Ray, you were just meant to poke around in my business a little, not to find anything."

He glanced at Tom and shook his head.

"When the Dabneys want a cop, we know where to find one. Honestly, Ray, what were you thinking?"

"I work for your uncle, not for you. Get on with it."

"Okay. The cat's nearly out of the bag, anyway. Listen, you two. I know more about May Blackburn's little operation than I've let on, and right now I see no reason to protect her. So I was thinking. What if I were to tell all that I know? What if I did that?"

Ray said, "I can't really see any harm in that, Dabney. The old man wants me to give him a report on her finances, as they relate to your missing assets. The more truthful you are, the more likely it seems you'll see some return on your losses. Assuming you've been defrauded, anyway."

"Thank you, Ray, but the question's more for Tom. As a policeman, what if I were to reveal to you some facts that

191

provided information about a crime? Would you have to tell your superiors where you got the information?"

"That depends. How serious a crime?"

"People have died."

"Murdered?"

"I don't really know. That might be an academic point. Is it a crime to conceal a natural death?"

"Maybe not. Look, Dabney, why don't you just clear your conscience and we'll figure it out as we go? I'm not here to charge you with anything. I'm not even on duty. I'm only trying to help a friend out with a little business trouble. As long as you don't tell me anything that implicates you in a felony, I expect we can keep your involvement quiet."

"And if I do say all I know, will you not tell my uncle that I've been less than forthcoming? And Ray, will you not repeat any of those foolish things that May said back there?"

Tom shot Ray a hard look. Ray nodded.

"You've got my word, Dabney. So, what is it?"

"There's a girl buried under a cottage in Venice. And before that, they kept her body in Westlake. They always say they're going to bring her back to life, but I don't believe that anymore. Not sure I ever did. Anyway, she's down there, and it's really been bothering me."

"Jesus," whispered Ray.

192

Tom took the ruled notebook out of his inside pocket, flipped it open and licked the stub of his pencil. "Who is she?"

"Willa Rhoads. R-H-O-A-D-S. Lived with her foster parents in the house on Manhattan when I first started coming around to meetings. Just about the prettiest little thing you ever saw—until she got sick, that is."

"Uh huh. And when did she get sick?"

"This was around Thanksgiving of 1924. I remember that she missed the big dinner because she was feeling poorly. She took to her bed for some weeks. May practices a sort of Christian Science, so everybody was praying over her, and we all were assigned some special Concords meant to bring her back to health."

"This was a ritual you were supposed to perform?"

"That's right. Not our regular Concords, but something special that May made up for Willa's sake. Mine involved a willow basket. But that's not really important."

"Go on. The girl was sick and people were praying for her."

"Yes. But she didn't get better. Her foster mother wanted to call in a doctor, but May wouldn't allow it. They had quite a row—as much of a row as anyone can have with May—and then both Mr. and Mrs. Rhoads were sent up to Oregon to reclaim some books that had been left behind at their old camp. May said having the books under the roof would help Willa get better. But by the time the Rhoadses got back to town with the books, Willa had died."

"And what then?"

"May called some of us into the chapel to break the news. I was there, and Ruth, Ward and Walter, Mrs. Turner and that druggist, Mrs. Sandusky. And of course the Rhoadses, poor souls, and Sammie. And May's old mother, who they got out of bed to attend. Eleven in all."

He closed his eyes, then conjured the scene. "Willa was laid out on a table, surrounded with flowers and branches. Her little face was thin and blue, and she was naked, with flowers on her sex. Someone had washed and curled her hair. There was a gold disc on her forehead and a pen in her hand."

He opened his eyes and addressed Tom. "I hope you're writing all this down. I'm not going to say it twice."

"Go on."

"May stood by the head of the body, and she gathered us in a circle, and told us that we represented the Divine Order Of The Royal Arms Of The Great Eleven, and that so long as we eleven held our tongues, the angels would be pleased, the Great Work would proceed as planned, and Willa would be waiting on the far side of the river just as we had known her, ready to be revived when the vibrations reached their

194

pinnacle. And also, we would all be richer than kings. May told us to twine our arms across the body and to take a vow to protect each other and the Great Work. She told us to kiss the girl and we did—"

Ray blanched. "Good God, man. How could you do that?"

"You heard May speak. You know how convincing she can be. We all did what she asked us to do. It seemed right. Anyway, she hadn't been dead long. She wasn't rotten! So we were all of us together, embracing over the body and making our vow. We thought by doing this, Willa could come back. Like the early Christians, like Jesus. She needed us, it seemed like. Wouldn't you have done the same?"

"I don't know. I'm not religious." Ray finished his drink with a grimace, then started in on Tom's untouched glass. "I'd rather you didn't ask me, if it's all the same to you."

Tom tapped his pencil on the notebook. "Dabney, after you took your vow, what happened to the body?"

"I'm not sure. May sent us all away and closed up the house with just she and her family in it. From what I heard and saw later, it seems they tried to mummify her along the Egyptian lines. I didn't see Willa again for some days, and when I did, she was in a big metal tub in the kitchen, heaped 'round with ice and salt and looking dry and brown. May called us all together to renew our vows and assist Willa's spirit in leaving the house with her body, as it went to its new abode."

"Then they took her to this place in Venice?"

"Oh, no, that was later. The Rhoadses went to stay in their own house nearby, so we all helped move Willa there. Then later on, when they moved on down to Venice, we did it again."

"How much later on?"

"A year and a few months, if I recall."

"So the body was disinterred to go to Venice?"

"Oh, God no. At the first place they kept her in the fish pond, under a tarpaulin, with fresh ice and more salt, and her dogs. She wasn't properly buried until Venice. No, well, she wasn't ever properly buried, but that's when they put her in the ground. So, that's about it, and as I said, it's been bothering me. Surely you can do something about Willa? I think it would be nice if somebody did something."

Dabney, unburdened, smiled at the other men, got up and stretched. "Gee, I'm tired. I think I'll just go up to bed now, and one of you can bring Alice home in the morning. Let yourselves out. Have another drink if you like."

Tom stepped in front of Dabney. Dabney slowed and gave him a quizzical look. "Yes, Tom?"

"You can't just wash your hands of this. Go to bed. I need to talk with some people. I'll call on you tomorrow to continue this discussion, and to make some plans."

"Oh, for Chrissake—"

Ray stood, too. "Shut up, Dabney. Like he said, go to bed. I'll see you in the office at 10. We've been going through your books, and you're going to answer all my questions, with frankness and fullness."

"I want to talk to my wife—"

"Alice will be at the office, too. And you can start looking after your wife tomorrow. I've got one of my own, you know."

"It's disgusting. Lunacy." Ray kept rubbing his hands on his trousers as if there was something sticky on them that he couldn't get off. "But it's got to be all right. It can't possibly be true."

"Or it could be. People have done weirder things, for weirder reasons. Anyway, there's one sure way to find out—"

Ray blanched and gagged. Tom laughed, mirthless and quick, behind the wheel.

"Oh, don't worry, you don't have to help dig her up. Let's go talk with someone, though. You're not tired, are you?"

"I think I won't sleep for a long time."

"That's fine. Frank Nance doesn't sleep much, either."

The County Morgue was at the very bottom of the Hall of Justice, a cool, quiet place where man's cruelty towards his fellows could be properly cataloged, its gentle technicians performing final ablutions, trocar sticks and tissue smears. Tom knew the back way in. At his knock, the boss man put his work aside and made them welcome in his tidy office.

Coroner Nance was a neat little person with slick dark hair, a round, boyish face and delicate spectacles that he had a habit of removing and balancing on the tip of his finger when he was thinking. His glasses were teetering precariously above his desk blotter as Tom explained their late-night visit and the possibility that a child's body had been illegally secreted and subject to years of peculiar rituals.

"Hmm. Hmmm-hmm." Nance spun the lenses in his hand and popped them onto his nose. "It's an interesting story, Tom. True or not, it's one I must, you understand, look into."

"We hoped you would. But there is the matter of—

"Yes, I know. Of course, Mr. Joseph Dabney wishes this to be handled discretely. That's fine, fine. I know just the man for this job. Venice fellow, clever—and quiet."

He jotted something down and handed the folded sheet across the desk. "Call this number in the morning, and ask for Horace. He'll be expecting you. As will I: full report, tomorrow evening, this time. If there's nothing to it, come see me all the same. I like the company of the living."

And he spun his chair away from his visitors, to the stack of glossy photographs of wounded flesh that had so distressed Ray upon arrival that he had spent the brief meeting tracking with great care the burned whorls of the cigar box at the front of Nance's desk and breathing, shallowly, through his mouth.

As Tom exchanged pleasantries with the elevator operator, Ray fiddled with his pipe stem. The halls were impersonal, too tall and too wide in the quiet of the night. Their steps clapped and echoed into the darkness beyond. Veins in the marble looked like hairs matted down in a stream of blood.

He remembered Muriel's red hair flying back from her face as the truck driver shoved her into the back of his truck, and the scratching of stones on his flanks as he threw himself down the hillside, away from Ward's avenging thrusts that hadn't come. The mountain smell, cinnamon dust and pollen. The gibbering fear rising in his belly, and Dabney's boney fingers clawing at the back of his trousers as they both tried to keep from falling further into the gorge.

Where the hell was she now? How had Dabney's idiotic pursuits brought them to this? How many more meetings, documents, how many more secrets until he could rest, hold her close again and be done with all of this madness?

He stopped and slumped against the cold wall, letting out a long sigh. Tom stopped and turned.

"What—what is it?"

"Nothing, but I need a drink. You go on. I'm going to Tony's."

"You need sleep. I'm taking you home to your wife."

Ray muttered a childish refusal, but didn't argue when Tom took his arm and led him down to the car and drove him home, waiting on the steps to make sure he went inside. The flat was dead quiet, no light under Cissy's door. Ray had a bottle of rye in his office, but he didn't go to it. His little bed, unmade and smelling of his own body, beckoned him down into the darkness where he slept, dreamless, well past dawn.

Sixteen

"Just hold tight," Muriel told Frank, as they stepped into the bright, modern Mayfair lobby with its mirrors, bustle and sharp angles. "I won't be long at all. You can get some coffee from Pat at the bar if you want."

He flopped down onto a long couch and waved her on.

It had been a long, strange night, but ultimately a pleasant one. After escaping down the mountain ahead of Ward's war charge and weathering a volley of rocks hurled by the little ladies who'd come out of their shacks in response to May's warning bell, the pair had raced across the valley floor, then back up into the hills and out to Malibu. There, after parking the distinctive truck out of sight behind a realtor's billboard, they'd hiked down to a little roadhouse Frank knew. Exhausted, their conversation crossing the winding pass had been sparse, but once they were perched in a cozy window booth, faces bathed in the fragrant mist of clam chowder—recommended by the waiter as just the thing for young lovers on a chilly summer night—like clams themselves, they soon opened up.

Between expressions of gratitude, Muriel explained her presence on the mountain, from the younger Dabney's asking his uncle for help, to her impulsive decision to follow the green truck through the valley, to Anna's approach at the walnut plant. She kept her narrative neat and professional—nothing in it about her complicated relationship with Ray or the awakening conscience which had troubled her since leaving Los Angeles.

Frank was more forthcoming. Having decided to help this strange girl and sever the cult's trust of him, his secrets came out, first in a trickle, and then—as their bellies were full, the fireplace crackled, and the waiter winked and sloshed two precise shots of whiskey from a trick tube up his cuff into their coffee cups—a rush.

Frank described how he had come to work for Mrs. May Blackburn after his brother Sammie, recently married to Ruth, failed to keep the regular Sunday dinner engagement in Alhambra. Their mother asked him to go to Los Angeles to see if Sammie was all right. But when he got there, Ruth, imperious, wouldn't even let him inside. When he asked to see his brother, she merely snapped that he had "gone away" and slammed the door.

"Did you go home then?"

"Gosh, no. Mother would have hit me with a spoon if I'd come back with that for an answer. I sat on the porch and waited, and every person who came or left that house, I asked about Sammie. Nobody would tell me anything, but I figured eventually someone would have to. And around nightfall, May Blackburn herself came out of the house and asked me to come inside."

Muriel breathed a low whistle and nodded for him to continue.

"I'd never met her, even though we were in-laws. Sammie had gotten out of the reformatory at Preston, having cleared his legal trouble up, and rather than coming straight home, he took up with Ruth. We just got a letter saying he was married, with a little photograph of the two of them at the courthouse. Then one time he brought Ruth to the house to meet Mother, and that was all. But I knew who May Blackburn was from Sammie's stories. I was surprised to see her, since he'd told me how reclusive she was. She brought me into the house and up the stairs and into a little room, and there was Ruth, sitting right in the middle at a little round table, all draped in a white lace shawl, and sort of sighing."

"Sounds dramatic."

"Oh, it was. She even had a spotlight on her. Anyway, May told me to have a seat opposite Ruth, and she slipped off somewhere leaving us alone. Then Ruth took out a folded up piece of paper and said she hadn't wanted to say anything to me, but that I was such a nice boy, and came from such a nice family. She didn't want to hurt us, but she didn't want us to worry either."

"About Sammie?"

"I guessed so. She wasn't making much sense. Finally she pushed the paper across to me and said I should read it. 'Dear Ruthie,' it said, 'I am so sorry that I have been so mean to you. I should have realized that after so many years of hard work that you have had in writing the Sixth Seal and the great sacrifices you have made that you were not strong and able to stand my abuse. This is good-by, from Sammie.' Naturally, I knew it wasn't my brother's handwriting, but I didn't say anything about that."

"Why not?

"Because I wanted to know what had happened to him. Even liars will tell you the truth if you sit back and let them talk."

"Very smart. What did she tell you?"

"Well, I asked her what had happened, and she said that on Friday she and Sammie has gotten into an argument about how much time she spent writing with her mother, and how they never went out any more and never had any fun. He said he was too young to sit up in the house all night doing nothing, and that he'd had enough. And she said he punched her in the stomach and pulled her hair and shoved her into the closet where he tried to make her put a party dress on."

"Oh! Would he do something like that?"

"He might have done. Sammie had a temper. He'd hit boys before, though I never knew him to hit a girl. Anyway, that's what she said, and I sort of believed her, because the way that girl talked could make anyone turn cuckoo. And it was after he'd hurt her and felt poorly about it, that was when she said he'd written this note and gone away in the middle of the night."

"Gone where?"

"She didn't know. Just that he took his things and fifty dollars, and that she hadn't seen or heard from him since."

"But he didn't write the letter?"

"No! Whoever wrote it didn't know how to use a pen properly, without smearing the ink. Sammie took pride in his penmanship, and always kept a nice pen in his pocket. And the words of it sounded sort of—I guess just stupid. I only saw it the one time so I can't say for certain, but I read it over several times, and I was pretty sure that it was written by a woman."

"That's right, you really can tell sometimes. So, what then?"

"Well, I didn't know what to do. I was pretty worried about Sammie, and it was plain I wasn't going to get anything else out of Ruth. But leaving didn't seem like it would help any. So I told her how sorry I was that my brother was such a brute, and that I hoped she was feeling all right now. She simpered some and told me that she was, although she'd had an awful stomach ache and had lost some hair where he pulled it.

I made nice, like—and then it struck me. It was just an impulse, really, but she fell for it. 'Oh, Miss Ruth,' I says to her, 'I don't know what my family's going to do now that Sammie's run off. He promised to get me a job with a man he knows, and we sure do need the money. Do you folks have any work for me? I'm strong, and hard-working, and much milder than my brother.'"

"You didn't really."

"I sure did! And they hired me as their chauffeur that very day—though that ratty old thing they called a car hardly deserved a driver. And so I didn't go home. I stayed, and I listened, and I looked for Sammie."

"Gosh. You didn't find him, though?"

"No, I never did. But I found his grip and all his clothes hidden back under some chairs in the basement, and that's when I knew for sure that their story about him running off was a lie. I felt pretty sure he was dead, but I couldn't

206

go home and tell our mother that, not without any proof. So I stayed on, hoping I might find something out about Sammie. I worked for them. And I saw some awful, awful things. And then today, I'd seen enough, and I helped you get away."

They stared at each other across the scarred wood table.

Outside, waves laced with phosphorescence crashed hard against the rocks. A wind had come up. The highway was empty. They were at the end of the world, suspended between the pagan city and the holy mountain, between their own fates and whatever paths they'd walked until they came upon each other in the cave. She reached across the table and took his hands in hers.

"Thank you, Frank, for saving me."

"You're very welcome, Muriel. It was my honor."

"I'm real sorry about your brother."

"Well, I can tell our mother now that he's not coming home. She'll be relieved, I guess. The hope has been the hardest part."

They sat quietly, warm and safe by the window. Then he began to talk again about life up in Harmony Hamlet, and the things he'd witnessed. Muriel asked some pointed questions about names, dates, sums and rituals, drawing out the details she'd need for the report she planned to submit to Joseph Dabney.

"Say, shouldn't you take some notes on all this business?" Frank wondered.

She just laughed and shook her head.

"What did I say that was funny?"

"Nothing. You'll understand when you get to know me better. Go on, Frank."

He did. His descriptions contained significant financial information, and she hoped it would be enough that her employer would forgive the loss, perhaps permanent, of the company Hupmobile.

As Frank spoke, a curious lightness came over him. From his first statements about individuals and their living and working situations, their travel and relationships, he began to laugh as he described yet more strange rites, and the funny things that May or Ruth had said, and his futile attempts to have sensible conversations with Ward on their long drives between Los Angeles and the mountain camp. Some of the stories were frightening, and he didn't laugh when describing missing persons or threats or animals being killed. But as the darker details were shared, he was able to recall other things, and marvel.

"My God, it's good to have someone to talk to—and not to have to hide who I am anymore."

Muriel nodded. "We've got all night if you want it. Tell me everything. I'd like to know it all."

As the first hint of dawn lit the eastern hills, they retrieved the truck and started back towards Los Angeles. The only other vehicles on the road were overloaded vegetable rigs coming in from Oxnard. The sea was smooth beneath a layer of mist. Muriel looked out over the bright band of air and fluid until her eyes ached, hoping to see a seal or a dolphin break the stillness. But nothing living showed itself, and she leaned her head on Frank's shoulder and dozed.

At Santa Monica they turned in towards the city, and he woke her for directions. She suggested they stop first at her hotel so she could change out of her torn and dirty dress, then continue on to the office. Near the Mayfair, he parked the distinctive truck in an alley, with the angel backed up against a disused loading dock.

"We'd better not take too long. May has a lot of friends on Crown Hill."

"Don't you fret. I'm a quick-change artist."

"I have five sisters. No girl I ever knew could say such a thing honestly."

"Well, you never knew me before, did you?"

"That's true, I never did."

She left him in the lobby and took Dan's elevator up to the 8th floor. He gave her the once-over in her ruined blue dress with its hem rudely dropped, but didn't razz her. They were old friends. His smile and soft "Hey now, Miss

Muriel, welcome home" felt like sunshine. It was good to be back.

Her suite was at the end of the hall, in the quiet part of the hotel where they put the monthly patrons. She heard the muted sounds of people preparing for the day inside their rooms. Her door was, surprisingly, locked twice. She fiddled with the deadbolt and stepped inside. The curtains were drawn and the dim room smelled of wine and apples. She wondered if Ray had been hiding out here on a drunk. It would be just like him to sneak away from his wife while she was off doing his job for him, to drown his misery in solitude and the grape.

But the bed, while rumpled, was empty. She snapped the bedside light on, opened the closet and selected a simple green rayon frock with a dropped waist and white piping, yellow shoes, a slip and stockings. She put the clothes on the bed, unzipped her dress, took her shoes off and stepped into the bathroom.

Alice Dabney was stretched out in the bathtub facing away from the door, with her long yellow hair draped over her arm and nearly scraping the floor. A mound of bubbles didn't obscure her small breasts. Her right hand was cupped between her thighs and she didn't hear Muriel enter. She did hear her shriek of outrage, followed by the slamming door and muffled cursing.

210

Furious, trembling, Muriel dressed, emptied her jewelry into her handbag, swept Ray's framed photograph off the bedside table and into the waste bin, then stormed from the room.

Alice, humiliated and shaken, huddled in the bathtub for some time before she dared get up, don Muriel's robe and peep into the bedroom. But at the door, she discovered that the key had been turned in the lock and withdrawn. She was trapped, not by May's followers, come to extract penance for her husband's indiscretions, but by Ray's lover, assuming Alice to be the same.

There was nothing she could do now but laugh and hang her stockings out the window in hopes that someone would see them flapping and release her. She sat on the toilet and flipped through the magazines on the rack beside. Ugh, deadly dullness. No fashion magazines or movie titles, or anything with pretty advertisements. She settled for an old issue of "The American Mercury," with Sherwood something-or-other going on about the talkies. It was better than nothing, but not by much.

"We're leaving," Muriel snapped over her shoulder.

Frank caught up with her outside on the sidewalk.

"Is everything all right?"

"Perfectly. Never more right in my life."

He had sisters, and knew when not to press.

Later, he lay on the cool leather daybed in Ray's office and listened while she read back his account of five years of pseudo-spiritual activity, financial exchange and human damage. Her notes were good, and hearing it all laid out so dispassionately made the fluttering terror in the back of his head grow quieter. Minor corrections were made, and then the final memo typed and handed to Joseph Dabney's secretary with instructions to give it to the old man as soon as he got to the office.

There was still no sign of Ray.

On his way to his mother's house, Frank dropped Muriel at the Barclay Hotel, where she took a room, bathed, and slept for a long time.

Seventeen

Marco Place was a dingy little street off Lincoln Boulevard. Modest pastel cottages draped with mildewed roses held the aggregated dreams and disappointments of retired postmasters, bank clerks, chicken ranchers, preachers and their wives, and spinster daughters. Doors and windows were shut tight against the clammy fog that ate family bibles down to the binding and left laundry to grow stiff and sour upon the line.

Here was a Cape Cod, here an English bungalow. A French Norman chateau shrunk down to miniature huddled entirely too close to a wee Spanish castle, the pitch of the first home's conical tower roof scraping against a browned cypress bush. Everything looked cheap and poorly finished. Five years ago, this had been scrub land.

Number 1094 wasn't any bigger than the others, but instead of sad roses it had a jaunty little palm tree, its lower trunk girded with fresh green moss. A pebbled path led up to the red studded door, set flush in a textured plaster that tried to evoke a Moorish walled garden, but only succeeded in looking like a service garage.

Horace Ridenour licked his thick thumb and buttoned up his jacket. "Okay, I think I got the picture. Let's see what they're hiding in there." He chuckled. "Probably a whole lot of nothing, but you've got the big man's interest up, so here we go."

They walked up the narrow path, stones sliding under their boots. Tom rapped smartly, and soon a little hatch within the door opened up and a rheumy blue eye peered through the grill. The eye darted around, taking in the two burly men standing on the stoop in the fog. It seemed in no hurry to shut the peephole or open the door. Horace went for his badge, but Tom shook his head. He leaned in close to the opening and brought his right eye in line with the hidden watcher's.

"Good morning, Mr. Rhoads. Is it Mr. Rhoads?" The eye froze, and blinked slowly. "May we come in, sir? We'd like to talk with you. It's important. It won't take but a moment." The eye bobbed once, and the little door slammed shut. Behind the door, they heard something heavy being dragged, and locks turning.

The door opened onto dimness. A tall gray man with thin hair parted in the center braced himself against the jamb. He had a crooked, hawkish nose and his smile showed more teeth on the right side. He blinked as if it had been some time since he'd seen daylight. When he spoke, he had an Iowa twang and a quaver.

"I am William Rhoads. What do you boys want?"

"We want to talk with you about Willa." Tom placed his foot inside the door in case Rhoads tried to push them out, but instead the old man gave a great sigh before stepping out onto the stoop.

Pulling the door shut, he breathed "Thank God you've come. Keep your voices down. My wife wouldn't want me talking, not about Willa and not to policemen. You are policemen, aren't you? I thought so, yes. But I've just got to talk with someone. I can't stand it any more."

"Go ahead," Tom said. "We're good listeners."

"Yes, yes. But oh, hey—are you here to arrest me?"

Horace snorted. "Nah, this one's working a private case on the side, and me, I'm off duty. You've got some big shots interested in your business, and we're just the advance party. Tell us what's cooking, we go back and tell the big shots. No problem for you, no problem for me. How's that sound?"

"That sounds—unlikely. No, I don't like the sound of that at all." He looked from Horace to Tom and to Horace again, hesitated, then turned back towards the house.

Tom caught his wrist and stopped him. "It's the truth, Mr. Rhoads. I am a policeman, in Los Angeles, but at the moment I'm just gathering information regarding Clifford Dabney. I believe you know him, yes? Detective Ridenour is stationed here in Venice. There's no crime here that we know of. All we want to do right now is ask some questions. And if I can be as bold as to say so, you look like you could stand to talk to somebody."

After a pause, Rhoads nodded. "Lord, that's true enough. I knew somebody would come, some day. It may as well be you two, now." He threw his head back and breathed the morning mist through thin nostrils. "My wife is going to the shops in a spell. You come back in half an hour. We'll talk about it then." He shook Tom's hand off, less timid for his decision. "Go on, git."

Tom and Horace got. They sat in Tom's car, and watched the door at 1094. After a time, it opened and a tall, sour-looking woman in a brown house dress and a white cloche stepped out. She had a basket over her left elbow. Tom recognized her from Manhattan Place. She trudged down the pebbled path and turned towards Lincoln Boulevard.

They watched her round the corner, then returned to the house. William Rhoads was standing in the doorway. The fog was burning off.

"Come on inside and sit down. I've been thinking it's a fine sort of day for putting old secrets to rest."

The front of the cottage was wide and dark with the impersonal air of a waiting room. A heavy curtain blocked access to the back of the house. Rhoads fiddled with a floor lamp, which cast a gloomy sort of brightness in a pool on the floor.

The only place to sit was a walnut pew, flush against the front wall. Tom and Horace stood awkwardly until Rhoads made an impatient gesture. They sat then, and the old man lowered himself smoothly to the rug and coiled his legs up into a startling pretzel twist. He placed both palms upright on his thighs, straightened his spine and began.

"You say you want to know about Willa, but I guess I'd better begin with May Otis—May Blackburn, rather. It was up in Klamath Falls that we took up with her, Lord, twenty years ago come spring. The wife and I had a little business healing the sick through prayer and diet, and May was at the time developing her own organization."

It was as though he'd been waiting for years to talk, and nothing would stop him until the story was out.

"We felt sympathetically towards one another. It seemed fine that we might go in together on the rental of a hall and various supplies. So our friends and her friends mingled some, and before long we all moved together to a place outside of town, where we could practice our respective faiths without interference from those that couldn't understand. That's the American way, is it not? Well, we soon came to find that there wasn't room for but one faith in May's mind.

But as it happened, Martha never was ambitious where such things were concerned, nor was I. And when May brought this little baby in and asked us to look after it, the fact was that Martha became quite preoccupied and let her healing slide. That was Willa."

He paused, did something fussy with his arms behind his back, then bowed while raising them, twined at the wrist, into an apex above his head.

Tom broke the awkward silence with a question. "Was she your only child?"

Rhoads looked up and swung his head. "No, no. We had a lot of children among us. Look—don't interrupt me. Do you want to hear about Willa or not?"

"I'm sorry, sir. Please go on."

"Fine. Listen, I don't know if you know May, but she can be prickly when you first meet her. Her mind is going a mile a minute, with the Great Work and all. So the basic courtesies can be overlooked. But once you know May, you love her. We all do—did. So me and the wife, we made it our business to make good friends for May, bring them in to the community where they could see her as she really was. Quite a few of these folks stayed on with us. Oh, it's a fine thing to have a big family. Do you boys have families?"

Horace nodded. "Two boys."

Tom said, "No sir. No living kin."

218

Rhoads let out a small bark. "Family isn't blood, son! Lord, if I counted only my own blood as my family, why, not even my wife would qualify. Got a no-count cousin, Elias, back in Merrill, he's a drunk and dumb as a stick. Don't call him family. But Willa, we raised that child from a tiny sprout and poured all our love into her, so she was our own. Oh, Willa! I wish you could have seen her. Prettiest little thing, cute as a bug when she was a babe, and grew up into such a fine little lady. Sometimes I would just watch her while she was sleeping and wonder how it was that such a pretty girl could be our daughter. Martha and me, we've never been much to look at, and when we first married she did worry that any child of ours might have my nose or her forehead and downturned eyes. Come to find out the Lord didn't care to bless us in that way, so it was fretting over nothing. But came Willa, and she was everything a mother could want. Not just pretty—she was good! She could sing, and was so helpful, and loved to kiss and cuddle. Yes, she helped us bring lambs into the fold. She was our daughter, but I reckon everybody she knew loved her like their own."

He shook his head wonderingly, and sighed. "Oh, that poor child."

"What happened to her, Mr. Rhoads?"

"She was so strong. See, we lost a lot of babies up in Oregon, you know how the winters are. My wife would pray hard, but it wasn't enough sometimes, or the Lord had plans. Oh, the Lord had plans. Buried those sweet lambs in the soil and the rock out in the hills and we'd come back in the spring and Willa would put bunches of flowers down for her dead friends. She never forgot them in her prayers, every night it was 'Bless Ida and Tommy and baby Marylee.' She'd talk to them, too, as if they were still alive. But she never was sick a day, not even when the rest of us were down with the 'flu in '17. Oh, that girl, she took care of the whole family, cooked us a broth standing up on a chair at the stove. That was Willa."

"She passed?"

"She passed. It was the end of November, nineteen and twenty-four. She had a little twinge in her back tooth, and so we prayed over her hard, and she said she felt the spirit in her. But she didn't get better, although she hated to complain. It was a busy time for all of us, because May and Ruth were making big headway with the Great Work, and the two of them would come down after transcribing all night and the rest of us would gather around them and pour all of our love energy in to fill them back up, so as they could sleep and get up again the next night to heed the angel's call. And we all of us had strong Concords that season, which had us criss-crossing the city to ensure each day's work was done before the angel returned. We'd moved to Los Angeles by

220

then, you see, because it had angels in its name. Angels. We should've stayed in Merrill."

"Her tooth got worse?"

"Prayer didn't help. Her jaw was swollen out past her ear, and she was in such pain. All she could do was suck on ice by the end. By the end—no, we didn't see the end. See, Martha wanted to bring a doctor in, even her faith was such that when she saw that prayer didn't help her baby she was willing to give modern medicine a chance. But May said no, there was still something we hadn't tried. There was a box of books we'd buried out behind the old place, to stake our claim on the mind of the soil. We were meant to go back up to Merrill and reclaim that box, to bring the mind of the soil to the city of angels where the sky and the earth and the sea would meet. May bought our tickets and took us to the train and told us not to worry, that she and Ruth would look after Willa while we were away."

He shuddered, and his face twisted up. He ground his fists into the carpet and shook his head hard several times.

"Mr. Rhoads, is there something I can get you?"

"No, I'll be all right. Please, excuse me. I have never spoken of this to anyone. It's a hard thing to tell."

"You're doing fine, sir. Take your time and tell it your own way."

"I think it's easier now if you ask me questions."

"Okay. Did you make it up to Merrill?"

"We did. And borrowed a pick from a neighbor, and dug up that box. It was locked. It wasn't heavy. There only seemed to be a couple of things in it, that rattled around loose-like. We took it down to the station and set off for Los Angeles on the next train."

"Were you met?"

"Yes. May's daughter Ruth came alone. We asked her to take us straight to Willa, but she took us up to the Mount Lowe tavern on the car instead. Said we had an important Concord that had been assigned by the angel Gabriel that very day. We didn't dare argue with her. Oh, Martha was not well. She was crying most of the way up the mountain, sick with a headache and worried for Willa. Ruth told us not to ask her any questions, but to pray silently as we rose. She kicked Martha something fierce for wailing. And when we got to the top, she made us carry that box out into a circle of trees and scratch out a hole with a stick. It took a long time, and Ruth just sat on a rock and watched us work. When the hole was dug, Ruth put something wrapped up in a handkerchief down at the bottom, and directed me to set the box on top of it. Then I covered it up with dirt and leaves and we went back down to town. It was only then that Ruth told us that Willa was dead."

"When was this?"

"New Years Day, 1925."

"Did you see your daughter again?"

"Oh, yes, sir. We saw her. When we got to the prayer house she was laid out on a table, so skinny and blue, and May said that bringing her back was going to be our greatest accomplishment as a faith. She said if we prayed hard enough, Willa would be redeemed and everyone alive would know what the Divine Order could do."

"Did you believe it, Mr. Rhoads?"

"For my wife's sake, I tried. Most of our lives together she's been the one with the greatest faith, and I've been happy to follow in her wake. Well, this thing was so awful, it seemed cruel to say a word against it. Questioning wouldn't bring our baby back. And for a time, I hoped maybe it was true. Wouldn't you?"

"You'd had a great shock."

"Oh, you wouldn't?"

Tom sighed. "The Lord never gave me such a challenge to my faith, sir. I cannot know. Nobody can know how they would react to such a trial."

"You're right. Nobody can know. Only Martha and I know what it's been like—not even the others in our club felt what we did. Certainly not May and Ruth. To them, her death was just a piece of the puzzle. A station of the cross.

And it's funny how, once Willa was stilled, the wealth flowed in and changed everything."

"Clifford Dabney's money?"

"Not just his, but yes. A number of newly faithful were drawn in around that time. It seemed as if our ladies burned with a brighter flame. Their lectures were so passionate. Before, maybe a hundred souls would pass through the doors for each one who truly took an interest, but afterwards, many people would come back and bring their friends, and pay for Concords, and leave gifts. And once we had Harmony Hamlet, there was a place for the lonely ones to go. To feel part of a family again."

"Do you know where the money was kept?"

"Sometimes I drove May to the bank. She had a lot of them. Not in town, out in the country around Harmony Hamlet. Let me think: in Oxnard, and San Fernando. And Zelzah. Oh, and in Newhall. And I think she had one in Pasadena, too."

"Did you live up there, at Harmony Hamlet?"

"No, sir. We visited, of course, but our Concord forbade us leaving Willa for long."

"Leaving Willa—? You stayed with her?"

"Yes. May did some particular things to her body, meant to protect the soul until the Great Work was finished and the secret of eternal life revealed. Then we were instructed in how to maintain the body until that time. We have looked after our daughter since that day."

"I understand. And would you say anything changed after Willa passed, in how you were in the community?"

The old man thought for a moment, then nodded.

"Ayuh, it was like they didn't want us around anymore. I didn't mind that. My patience with all the Concords and foolishness had grown thin. There was an incident up at Harmony Hamlet that sealed it. All the people were sitting in the cookhouse, hungry, as May oversaw the sacrifice of six hundred of what she called sacred chickens. She stood in a circle of the dead birds and took their heads and put them all together in a bag and shook them up, saying they'd bring divine inspiration home to her."

"Gracious. And you ate the birds after?"

"Lord, no. She burned them to ash while Ruth danced around the fire in her Egyptian costume."

"That seems wasteful, and mean."

"Yes, but that wasn't even what bothered me. It was the chickens themselves, you see."

"The chickens?"

"May sent me out to Van Nuys to buy them, gave me a big stack of money. Lord, the smell and the noise and the heat in that truck. I must have visited three dozen ranches before I had what she wanted. See, she insisted that they all

225

had to be Rhode Island Reds. It wasn't until I'd named that breed the last time that it struck me: Rhode. Rhoads. I'll be honest: I got scared, Mr. James. I told Martha we'd do best to stay around town, and we have."

"Here. With Willa?"

"Yes, she's here, too. Come." He stood, knees popping as he rose, "Would you like to see her?"

Behind the thick curtain, the back of the house was open and airy. They passed through a little kitchen, bright with green and yellow tile and a gay linoleum carpet, down a hall with a telephone alcove and lilac bathroom, then left into a surprisingly large and sunny bedroom, the back wall of which must touch, or nearly touch, the property line. It was furnished in sober, masculine Mission furnishings and smelled overwhelmingly of cedar.

Rhoads took one end of a chest at the end of the bed and heaved it up. Horace stepped in to help. They carried the box over to the window and put it down. Rhoads rolled the Turkish carpet in from the wall up to the bed. Underneath, a neat, wide trap door was set flush to the floorboards, with a clever recessed locking mechanism at the side. He found the key on a ring from his pocket.

"Hey, that's nice," observed Horace, meaning the hatch.

"There's no point in doing something poorly."

"You're a cabinetmaker?"

226

"Lumberman. Sawmill. Back in Oregon. Anyway, she's down here. You sure you want to see?"

"We're sure. Open it."

Rhoads knelt, turned the key, moved aside and pushed. The door slid into a pocket, revealing a dark pit that gave off the scent of the sea and another big waft of cedar. Nervously, Tom and Horace approached the hole. They crouched and peered in. Rhoads snapped the light switch, and the overhead bulb illuminated what was there.

Down in the wet Venice soil, a pair of metal-wrapped wooden trunks of similar size were set at precise angles, one centered in the hole, the other nearer to the bed.

Rhoads lowered himself into the pit, crouched, and opened the central box.

Willa Rhoads lay curled on her side, knees drawn up, head tucked down. She had been a small girl, and she was smaller in death. Her skin was brown and desiccated, but the fineness of her features was still evident in profile. Colored rocks and powder were heaped up around her corpse, and pooled in the folds of her shroud. Rhoads brushed a bit of mildew from her ear with gentle fingers. Her hair was curled, her hands folded in prayer. Horace crossed himself. The room felt very big and very old.

Tom's hand went to the inside of his coat, where the girl's photograph was safely tucked between the pages of his beat notebook. "God bless this child," he whispered.

"God bless us all," William Rhoads answered. "Help me get her out of here."

"Sir?"

"I can't live like this anymore. The child needs a proper grave, with her name on it. Up in the sun, under grass. Maybe some roses blooming near. A place where I can rest, too, when my time comes. Soon enough, oh soon enough. Martha and I won't be here forever—and a child shouldn't die before its parents. Boys, it's a terrible burden, to live tethered to a tomb. Nobody could ever understand."

"We have to report this," said Tom. "There's going to be an inquest."

"I know. I've been waiting a long time for someone to come. Funny it's that fool Dabney sets it all in motion. But you can't ever tell who's going to be important in your life, can you?"

Tom shook his head, and put his hand down into the hole. "Come on up, Mr. Rhoads. There are men whose job it is to bring your daughter into the light."

The old man sighed and closed the casket. "All right."

Then, once the hatch was shut, a quiet question seeking no reply. "D'ya think I'll be able to sleep again, once she has gone?"

Tom left Rhoads and Horace in the kitchen and went down to the corner to telephone Coroner Nance. He'd gone home and it took a while to reach him. When he did, Nance told him to sit tight. Coming back down Marco, Tom heard noises coming from the open door of 1094. Martha Rhoads had returned, and she had collapsed on the living room floor. She was sobbing. Her husband knelt, half wrapped around her, muttering small entreaties for calm. Horace was at the kitchen door, face turned away.

The woman sensed him above her and leveled a red, wet stare at the newcomer.

Tom, not knowing how else to respond, smiled.

Martha smiled, too. She shook her husband off, stood up, and stalked across the floor. She was still grinning when she spat in Tom's face.

"I knew you were a fake! Go ahead, flatfoot," she smirked. "Desecrate the belief I have. Take Willa's life away forever— dig up the body! What do you care? I can't stop you, and he—" she pointed an accusing claw at Rhoads, "he won't even try."

She wrapped her arms around her shoulders and shook in mute fury, then began again. "Bullies and cowards, all I've ever known. Willa was better than this world, and now she won't ever come back to it. Fine! I won't stay long either— just you watch, William Rhoads, just you watch!"

She moved towards the back of the house and Horace put his hands out to stop her. She pushed him aside and he folded.

"Mrs. Rhoads—?"

She was crying again, big shining tears that rolled into the creases around her rigid lips.

"I know it's done now. You don't have to worry about me. Come into the kitchen, boys. I'll boil some coffee while we wait."

They sat with her there in awkward silence til the wagon came, and drank all the good coffee she poured them.

Willa came out of the ground with a hungry, sucking sound. The other casket came easier, the ground wetter for her loss. Nance had given orders that both boxes be brought downtown just as they were. Two strong men laid white sheets on the carpet, wrapped them up, and trundled their quarry into the back of the ambulance.

Mrs. Rhoads stood dry-eyed in the front yard, watching them work. She had no reaction as the first chain-wrapped box was carried out, but the second, taller in their arms, elicited a terrible cry. She sunk against the palm tree, her hands working furiously in the moss, her mouth gaping in an arid O. Her husband stood near, muttering small soothing words that went unnoticed, and then he, too began to howl.

"God. God. God. Willllllaaaaaaaaaaa."

Tom couldn't stand it. He climbed into the ambulance and rode back to the city with its tender cargo.

Later, Tom stood by the morgue's high windows, hands laced behind in his patrolman's posture. On the metal table, illuminated in a bright triangle of light, lay the brown, dry figure of the long-preserved child. Dr. Wagner was crouched beside her, methodically making his way around the body, paying particular attention to the seam running like a Y from each shoulder down to the belly, split but not gaping.

The fat little man was quick and limber. He rolled on his heels, scanning the form before him. His pencil stub flew across the notebook in his palm. He grunted.

With gentle hands in soft gloves, he turned the body over on the table, saw something that interested him and dipped in for a closer look. He took something like a leaf or a fabric scrap off the hip with a long pair of tweezers and dropped it into a jar.

Taking up a metal implement, he pushed hair away from the shriveled face, came in close, and sniffed deeply. He hummed.

"Any idea what killed her, Doc?"

"Huh?"

His reverie broken, Wagner straightened and shook his head.

"No, no. Not yet. She's in good condition—considering—but she's been a long time in the salt water. It'll likely come down to a chemical analysis, not that that's any guarantee of an answer. I can tell you a few things that didn't kill her, but nobody ever wants to hear me tell them that."

"I do. What didn't kill her?"

"Wasn't strangulation." He tapped towards the neck with his metal rod, a conductor playing an elegy. "She didn't drown, either. No sign of poisoning, though it doesn't leave signs always. She wasn't in a fire. No bones broken. Not shot or stabbed. Not strangled, but I can't say she wasn't smothered. But these—" he gestured across the room to a second table, where the bodies of seven small dogs lay on their sides, back to belly, noses pointed north—"these little creatures were poisoned. With ether."

"You can tell that after all this time?"

"Oh yes. Whoever did it left the cone in the trunk. And a hint of the smell remains, I think. So the dogs were killed, and put into the same stuff she was in, to look at them. And kept close to her for quite some time, before they went into their own box."

"How d'ya know that?"

"She's covered in their hair. And come, look at this—"
He swooped back towards the girl, rod extended towards the
left side of her abdomen. "D'ya see that?"

Tom unhooked his hands and stepped slowly towards
the body, keeping a bit of distance from the table's edge.
He dipped his head.

"What am I looking for?"

"Closer, man! Here, d'ya see this shape, a little point
here, and here, and another here, and then the roundish
bit?"

'Yeah, I see it. What's that, then?"

"It's the imprint of that brown and white one's back left
paw—pointing down, see? And here's a little bit of his tail,
curled just as you can see it still."

"Oh. Oh."

Tom stepped back involuntarily. He was a cop. Bodies
didn't bother him. They were mere information to be read
and recorded. But now he saw the pretty child of the picture,
heaped in a pile of dirty dogs, their bellies pressed against
hers, and he felt the room pitch beneath his feet.

He went to the water cooler and poured himself a cup,
then another, and drank, his shoulder pressed against the
wall.

When he had collected himself, he saw that Wagner was
absorbed in something under the microscope by the windows. The scientist scarcely looked up when Tom said he

233

was going out to get some air. He didn't turn when Tom felt something small beneath his shoe, bent, and took it up. It was a little cracked tooth that had rolled from the table onto the floor. Without knowing why, he pocketed it.

The hall outside was empty. Tom took the stairs and stepped out onto the grassy plaza. The day already promised to be another scorcher. He crossed to the steps of the old sandstone courthouse and went inside. Midway down the hall, in a short L, the freight elevator stood open. A wheeled basket piled with papers was half inside. Nobody was around.

Tom pulled the cart out, closed the gate, and rode up to the 9th floor. It was another short flight to the flat roof capped by slim towers with the fat red dome above. Leo, the caretaker, kept pigeons here. There was a good leather chair, formerly a judge's, under a green striped awning, with an ottoman to match.

Tom plopped down. It was a fine place to sit and think, or to get away from his thoughts.

Below, the hum of the city was distant and regular. The big clock in the tower contributed its even burble of clacks and whirrs.

Up here, above the world, it was better than below. No one could see his face, which felt tender and exposed. There was a slight breeze, and a solitary peregrine, tail splayed, rode on it. It wasn't hunting, but just delighting in the air.

The fat rollers cooed and pushed together in their loft. He took Willa's photograph out of his pocket and laid it on the ottoman, leaning forward to study her face.

Pretty, so pretty—but ruined for him now. Soft cheeks gone furrowed, plump lips dry and pulled back from the gums, eyes sunken behind powdery lids, curls matted with fluids unnamable. A naked dog against her naked belly. Her death merely a lever spilling cash into a madwoman's pockets. The centerpiece of hideous rites. Unknown and unrecorded.

There were things worse than growing old.

He shuddered, and sighed, and flipped the photo over on its face.

"She ain't worth it, pal," came a sly whine from some place above and to his left.

Tom kicked the bench away and wheeled around.

A slim young man with a nose like a new potato peered down at him from a square platform set onto a pole near the edge of the roof. The stranger laughed.

"Sorry if I spooked you. But you had a look like you might wanna jump—not that it's any of my business, but if you jump from my roof, it is my business."

"I'm not going to jump."

"Glad to hear it, chum. Jumping solves nothing."

"Jumping—I'm not—ah—who in blazes are you, anyway?"

235

"Me? They call me 'Perch' Pattison, King of the Pole—or they will, once I set the record. Right now I'm just getting warmed up."

"Sure. You're one of those flagpole sitters. Endurance men. You that fella who was up on top of the dance hall, fella with the cork hat?"

"That amateur? Nah. I'm gonna leave him in the dust, though. Watch this!" He cinched his belt, leaned forward, tucked his neck down and performed a headstand, casting his legs and arms out into a jaunty X.

"Never see anything like that before, didja?" the man gasped, through reddening cheeks.

They were very high up, and now Tom felt the height. The noise of the city rose up with a discordant blare.

"No, I never did. Will you please sit back down?"

"Sure, sure." The acrobat unfurled himself and planted his bottom on the platform, legs swinging. "Is that better?"

"That's better."

Pattison grinned and licked his lips. "So, she your girl?"

"No, she's not my girl."

Pattison scratched himself. "So that's the problem. Listen pal, there are a million girls. The sooner you start to forget her, the sooner you start to be happy."

"So you're a philosopher on a perch."

"I know about people."

"Yeah? Tell me about people."

"Do me a favor first."

"What favor?"

"Can you dump this for me, down that drain there?" Without waiting for an answer, he started lowering a battered red coffee tin tied at three corners with dirty twine.

The contents sloshed as the tin hit the roof, and Tom screwed up his face and backed away.

"Come on, please? It's getting awful ripe up here."

"Fine, fine." The twine was long enough to reach the drain, barely. "What were you going to do if I didn't come along?"

"Toss it out over the edge, probably. But you're a cop, aren't you? And that would be against the hygiene code. You are a cop, right?"

"Yeah, I'm a cop." He poured the piss away.

"I thought you were. Listen, I'm not a public nuisance. You can't see me from the street at all. And Leo said I can be here."

"I don't care what you do. Just don't turn any more tricks. Go on, tell me about people."

"Okay, go on back to the edge. See the streetcar?"

Tom obliged him.

"See? Streetcar pulls up, people get out, all kinds of people. Men, women, old people, kids. Everybody's got a story, and to every one of them it's the most important story in the world. Hurry hurry hurry, down the sidewalk and into an office building, then out again later. Rush rush rush. Off to school, off to work, home to the family, zip zip zip. Fall in a mud puddle or fall in love, hit the jackpot or get hit by streetcar. Ambulance comes, carts 'em away. None of it matters. They only think they're special, but they're not."

"That's how it looks to you, eh? How long you been up on that thing?"

"Long enough. I knew a thing or two before I climbed up here, but listen, you sit here a couple of days, and it all becomes plenty clear. I sit, and I watch, and I see it all. Some of 'em come in couples into the courthouse, take the honeymoon elevator up, ride down as man and wife. You can tell just watching how they walk together if they're wasting their time. I see those types come back, separate like, go up to the courtroom and try to kill each other—legally, I mean. I guess that makes the world go round. Up here, they're all the same. Who needs people?

"The sun comes up and it's just me and him, and he's hot and he's beautiful, and different every day. I can almost look at him, through my fingers. The moon comes up, and it's just me and her, all night long, and she's glad to be looked at. She's perfect, and cold. I don't expect a damn thing else, and man, she delivers. Down there, it's just sweat and trouble. Up here, you know what you're in for. No surprises."

"No surprises."

"Anyway, I'm glad you're not gonna jump. Leo lets me practice up here, but he'd be real mad if I let anybody hop off his roof."

"I'll tell you what, 'Perch.' I'm just going to sit here. And you're going to be very quiet, like you were before I noticed you. And in a little while, I'm going to leave you here with your pee can and Leo's pigeons and your stupid ideas. How does that sound?"

"That sounds just thrilling. Ducky." He turned his back and curled up like a boy, pouting.

But he didn't say anything else, and Tom was able to put his thoughts back together.

And when he didn't feel so raw, he left the roof and took a train out to Manhattan Place, where a credulous oil man who didn't exist still had a date with a high priestess. Up on the roof, the slim man watched him go and wondered what his story was.

Eighteen

Now as for Alice Dabney, she wasn't trapped for long. Her makeshift flag caught a newsboy's eye, and a maid soon unlocked the bathroom door with an insinuating chuckle that enraged Alice. Her fear ripened to indignation, and there was no reasoning with her by the time Ray arrived. She didn't want to go to Dabney Oil, or to put Muriel's too-tight shoes on. She was hungry and bored and sick of being shifted around like the furniture.

He calmed her with the promise that if she just did what he asked she could go right home and change into her own things, the exaggeration that her husband was eager to see her, and the lie that all their problems with May Blackburn would soon be resolved.

She pouted but said all right, and he waited in the hall while she dressed and packed her few things.

Back on Oxford Avenue, he had to lean on the bell for a long time until Dabney, bleary in pajamas, opened up. He seemed surprised to see Alice but gave her a brief, brotherly embrace. She wiggled free and they all stood awkwardly in the hall.

"Hi, Alice. That's a nice dress."

"Thank you so much. It's not mine."

She glowered at him.

"I'm sure you two would like to catch up, but there isn't the time. Dabney, unlock your wife's closet, then get dressed yourself. And hurry up."

Driving downtown in heavy silence broken by his and hers sighs, Ray was conscious of his own marital unhappiness, like a stone in his throat. Why did people who hated one another feel compelled to cling unto death? He wished Warren Lloyd were still alive so he could ask him. Warren's insights into human behavior always cleaved through his own blind spots.

But Warren had loved his wife. And he had still died.

Now Alma was broken and alone, and the whole family shoved off-kilter.

And was it not in their home, with their encouragement, that he had taken up with his own bitter mate? Better, perhaps, not to love so much, to find some comforting middle ground. A zone of kindness and care, but no obsession, no rage, no tears, no lust, no need. Not that he'd ever known such a thing, but surely a love like that existed.

He knew that Cissy was in the apartment while he washed, shaved, dressed and made his own breakfast. He didn't hear, but he sensed her through the walls. Scanning the morning paper between bites of egg and fried tomato on rye toast, he felt the heat of her loathing like a second sun. But she didn't come out and he didn't go looking for her. Before he drove away he looked back and saw a curtain flick in the upstairs window. She'd miss him, he knew, in her way. Maybe, after this was all over, they could take a few days away together and lose themselves in newness.

His office smelled like Muriel, and he winced at her scent.

Pretending he'd only stepped in to collect his messages, he led his charges down the hall to the younger Dabney's office. There, Dabney simply went to the desk blotter, peeled back the paper, and handed over a typewritten record of his every economic transaction with the Blackburns.

"I didn't think you had it in you, Dabney. You've got business sense after all."

"I keep our books, Mr. Chandler," corrected Alice.

Dabney said nothing. Ray read.

The story of the relationship when spread over five years appeared as neutral and regular as the tides. A comfortable bank account inexorably emptied by regular withdrawals, called tithes in the ledger. An oil lease transferred, then two more. The bank account less comfortable. A car purchased and immediately signed over. Bills for building supplies. The conveyance of real property at Santa Susanna from a private citizen to a corporation. Bills from a print shop for small runs of pamphlets, self-covered and boxed. Costumes: Ruth. Groceries: Harmony Hamlet. Chickens and mules: sacrificial. And for several years, amounting to a startling total, daily deliveries of ice by the block, the orders larger from early summer and through the fall.

The little group sat together over the document, Ray interrogating, the Dabneys recounting—reluctantly, carelessly, quietly, but more or less completely, the story of their financial entanglements with May Blackburn and her cult.

Concerned about discretion, he moved to type the memo up himself, but Alice said she'd help. So he dictated and she typed, not badly, the short stack of pages that was the dry portrait of her family's descent into madness and loss. The switchboard girl said the old man was in a meeting. Ray stashed the finished memo in Dabney's desk.

"Well, we've done it. Now what?" asked Dabney.

"Until we get this matter tidied up, why don't the pair of you go away for a little while? As long as I can reach you with any questions, that seems best. The Del Coronado all right?"

Dabney lowered his eyes, and made a soft, deferent grunt.

"Of course, the company will cover your expenses. Go, swim and enjoy the sunshine, eat enchiladas. Don't worry about this affair. It will be better when you come back, once your uncle has called in some favors. I'll let you know when it's safe. All right?"

"Yes, that sounds nice. Thank you, Chandler. This has all been very difficult, but I want to—"

"Please, you don't have to say anything. I'm just doing my job."

He gave them some money, saw them off at the Pickwick Stages and stopped at the Athletic Club for lunch and a long steam. Some of the anxiety of the past days fell away. When he got back to his office, Muriel was sitting primly on her dictation chair, with her hands folded in her lap. She tipped her face up, slower than necessary, met his eyes, and performed a maneuver that had all the muscular components of a smile, but wasn't one.

"Oh, hello there, Ray," she trilled.

"Muriel."

"Surprised to see me?"

"Happy to see you. To see you all right."

"No thanks to you."

"No, no thanks to me. That young man on the mountain—"

"His name is Frank."

"Oh. Yes. I-I—" He shook his head and sat down. He seemed smaller than she'd remembered him, with a papery look around his eyes.

"I'm very sorry, Muriel. I was frightened. I hope you can forgive me for running away."

If she'd been angry when he entered, now she was only sad.

"For that, I suppose I can forgive you. But it's not really enough, is it? Today I forgive, tomorrow I forget, and next month or next week you hurt me all over again. Office girl, like the office car, efficient, reliable, undistinguished, utterly replaceable. 'Muriel, take a memo.' 'Yes, Mr. Chandler.' 'Muriel, go buy yourself something pretty.' 'Oh, thank you, Mr. Chandler.' 'Muriel, haul my ashes.' 'Of course, Mr. Chandler.'"

She shook her head.

"Ray, I'm done. You're a nice enough man, and you've been good to me, but I don't want to be anybody's pet."

"No. You deserve much better than this. Than me."

"Yes, I do. And you won't even miss me when I go. There will always be somebody else, another woman who needs a little of what you have so little to give. Another secretary who has to be nice to you, even if she wants to be."

She smiled at him, with as much love as he'd ever seen on her funny, almost-pretty face.

"You should try loving your wife, Ray. Maybe there's really nothing there to salvage, but how will you ever know if you don't try? You spend your life hiding from everything that matters to you, numbing yourself, being clever. Clever people aren't ever happy, are they?"

"I'm not clever. Nor happy. You never knew me at all."

"Maybe not. I don't care now. Anyway, you'll be all right. So will I. Here—"

She handed him a folded sheet of paper on South Basin Oil Company stationery. It was from him to her, unsigned, a letter of recommendation that would earn the presenter a top-flight secretarial position any place in the country. He read it over quietly, signed it and passed it back.

"Thank you. I think four week's severance is fair."

"Take six."

"All right. But—I lost the car."

"I did tell you to come home."

"I don't have a home. But I will, someday."

She kissed him, like a sister. He accepted, chaste, numb.

"The car isn't important. Dabney has plenty of cars."

"I know that. Will you try with Cissy?"

"I'll try to try."

She was leaving now. Why had he never noticed how perfect her ears were? Too late, too late.

"I hope you'll be happy, Muriel. Will you write to me?"

"I'll write when I'm happy, how's that? Good-bye, Ray. Send my pay care of General Delivery, Alhambra."

"Alhambra?"

But she was gone. He didn't stop to think about it. He instructed the accounting office to cut her final check, called the manager of the Del Coronado to ensure Clifford and Alice were properly taken care of, then got Lew on the line.

"You can cancel that missing persons report. I found the girl."

"Oh, that's fine. She all right?"

"She seems to be. Left a car up on the mountain, though. Hupmobile, dark red, registered to—"

"I know, I've got all that in her file. Want me to see if I can bring it back down?"

"Only if you think you can do it safely. There's a $50 reward, $75 if you need help, and I'll run you back out to the valley if you bring it home."

"Okay. I'll let you know. What did the girl have to say?"

"That she doesn't like the way I treat my wife."

"Oh, don't mind her. People are funny when they get scared. I'm sure she didn't mean it. Take her out to a show, she'll come 'round."

"Just call me, Lew."

"Yeah, okay."

Nineteen

The green bungalow was locked up tight, with no welcoming signs in the window. A single car was down at the end of the drive, half inside the garage. It had a dirty tarp draped over it. Tom stood on the porch, head cocked. He knocked again.

A heavy window opened above, and a languid voice coiled down. "Who's calling?"

He stepped back onto the second step and looked up.

Ruth Angeline Wieland Rizzio was leaning out onto the sill. She had wrapped herself up in the window curtains, and a pale flash near her center suggested they were all she was wearing. He forced himself to look at her eyes. They were kohl-rimmed and sleepy, with dark curls falling down. She was prettier than her photograph, with good color and a rough charisma.

She smiled. He smiled back.

"Miss Ruth, I presume? We have an appointment to meet today. My name is Tom James, and I am interested in taking up a subscription."

She clapped her hands, causing the curtains to quake all around her, and disappeared from the window. He stepped back onto the porch, and soon enough the lady herself, in a modest white robe and golden sandals, opened the door and welcomed him inside.

She had the manner of someone who had no truck with the social niceties, and simply did as she pleased. She led him through the hall, lightly up the steps, and into the plain bedroom he had explored previously. The room now contained a fancy Chinese bed shoved against the wall, heaped high with velvet pillows that spilled out onto the floor. A floor lamp was draped with sheer silk. The room was very hot.

"I hope you don't mind the informality," she simpered. "I am so much more comfortable reclining."

"You sit however you like, ma'am. But I'll need a hard chair."

She made an annoyed gesture and flitted out of the room, returning with a spindly, armless Windsor. He set it opposite her regal pile. He perched, she lounged, and they gazed at each other, spider and fly.

She broke the silence.

"Hello, Mr. James. Our William told me you'd come to hear about the Great Work. We're always thankful for the interest of careful souls."

249

Tom stretched his legs out and hummed encouragingly. She tucked her arms behind her head and turned one hip towards him. He had a flash of déjà vu, then recognized the pose from the artistic nudes sold behind the counters at the downtown phonograph parlors he'd rousted early in his career. Cheap reproductions of Italian masterpieces, the subjects goddesses but the models common whores. A cheap gesture, and one ill-suited for him. It did not have its intended effect.

But she didn't seem to care or notice.

"Soooo," she drawled, "Am I right to understand that you're particularly interested in mapping the pathways by which oil travels beneath the surface of the earthly crust?"

Tom nodded. "I surely am, Miss Ruth."

"Of course, such information will be revealed—when the Great Work is finished."

She smiled and nodded and waited for Tom to return the volley.

Tom felt suddenly heavy and old. He didn't care to grin at her again, or continue this tedious conversation about subscriptions and miraculous texts and pockets of hidden wealth, leading up, inevitably, to the attempted seduction and solicitation of funds to continue her literary efforts.

He was conscious of the quietness of the house, the smell of her violet perfume, the creepy doll laid out in the room beyond, and of Willa's little tooth in his breast pocket, slightly pinching at his heart.

"Why don't we cut out the small talk, Mrs. Rizzio?"

She started and came forward, trembling with rage that might be real. He stood and spread his arms. The door was behind him. Her small head darted round, a panicked bird in a stuffy velvet cage.

"Please sit down, miss. I'm not going to hurt you. We're just going to speak a spell."

She sat then, her face a mask of hatred with a hint of fear bleeding through.

"Speak? Whatever do you propose to speak with me about?"

"Honestly, miss, I'd just like to understand what you and your mother have been doing in my town. I've been chasing all over the country cleaning up your messes, finding more questions than answers, and I've simply had my fill. So let's you and me talk, and when I'm satisfied, I'll go."

"What are you," she sneered, "a journalist?"

"It doesn't matter what I am."

"Mother doesn't let me talk to journalists."

"Nothing you tell me is going to be published. You're just going to satisfy my curiosity. Or I can just satisfy it some other way."

"There's no need to insinuate, Mr. James—your name is Tom James, is it not?"

"Sure it is."

He didn't seem so tough to Ruth, but he wasn't moving, either.

"Oh, pooh! Fine, we'll talk. Hurry up. I'm bored with you."

She sprawled back on the bed, this time with her ankles crossed.

Tom dragged his chair back against the door and began.

"All right then. I'm going to tell you a story, and you'll fill in the gaps for me. Okey doke?"

Ruth yawned and checked her manicure.

"I know you were rooming with Opal Loomis in 1924, and dancing at the Love Land ballroom."

She snorted. "What if I was?"

"Are you ashamed?"

"I'm not ashamed of anything."

"What about the way you treated poor Arthur Osborne? Taking his money, leading him on?"

"Oh, good grief! He enjoyed himself—a whole lot. He loves to love me, and a man like that could never really have a woman like me."

"What kind of woman are you, Mrs. Rizzio?"

"Don't call me that!"

"Aren't you Mrs. Rizzio?"

"You tell me—you seem to know all about it."

"I know your husband Sammie's been gone a long time. Did your mother poison him, Mrs. Rizzio?"

"Certainly not! He left."

"A man left you?"

"I told him to go. He wasn't any help to us at all. So what? What's he to you, anyway?"

"I don't claim to understand all you and your mother have been up to since you came to Los Angeles, but it seems to me that you've caused a lot of bother, and that folks just seem to disappear around the two of you. Like Frances, for instance."

"Frances who?"

"I don't know her last name—not yet. But I know you put her into an oven, and she didn't come out of it."

"Do you know how ridiculous that sounds?"

"You deny it?"

"Certainly, I deny it. People don't go into ovens."

"If you're going to keep lying to me, Mrs. Rizzio, we're going to have to go about this another way."

He looked at her as if she was laid out in a butcher's window. His eyes slipped down her neck to her breasts, belly, legs. He was weirdly still, hardly breathing. He didn't lick his lips or show any signs of arousal. All he did was look at her with that funny flare around his nostrils and let his words die on the air.

She scuttled up against the back of the bed. Although she was the sort of woman who thought almost nothing of giving herself to a man, there was something wrong about this one. She didn't want him to touch her or even look at her with that awful, even stare. She didn't know what he wanted, and that frightened her. The only option seemed the one she'd never considered.

She could just tell a mark the truth and hope he'd go away.

"Okay, buster. What is it that you really want to know?"

He thought of Sammie, who was only a name and a ridiculous story about a dance on poisonous sands, and about someone called Frances—he knew not if she was fat or thin, young or old, cruel or kindly—baking away in some sort of hearth. They seemed unreal, and he couldn't force himself to care about their fates. Ruth seemed sympathetic, in this moment, to truthful revelations—not the kind she and her mother sold on street corners through a clownish factotum.

There was only one thing he really wanted to know.

"Tell me about Willa."

She sighed.

"Willa died."

"Before that. Who was she?"

"Willa? Willa was a little girl without parents who was taken in by our family. Up in Oregon. The Rhoadses took her as their daughter, and she helped us around the temple. She was a nice little girl. Then she took sick and she died, oh, some years ago."

She shrugged and looked at the door.

"And that's all of it?"

"No. That's not all of it! I know what you're getting at. We didn't report her death and we carried her around from place to place in advance of the resurrection. Last I heard, the Rhoadses had her. All right? I expect there's some law against it, but it's just what we happen to believe. Is that what you wanted me to tell you?"

"That's better. Do you really believe Willa's body can be resurrected?"

She laughed, a real laugh, and shook her head.

"Oh hell, who knows? I've seen stranger things, or as strange. It didn't hurt anyone, what we did with her. She was already dead, and it made people feel better to think it wasn't forever. It certainly soothed Martha Rhoads's heart— she loved the child. Haven't you ever prayed over a grave and wished somebody could come back?"

"Sure I have. What kind of sickness did Willa contract?"

"I don't know. Stomach something. Influenza."

"Which is it? Stomach something or influenza?"

"Influenza."

"Did anyone else take sick?"

"I don't remember. It was a long time ago."

"Were you sad when she died?"

"Sure I was."

"Why? Did you like Willa?"

"I liked her okay. I'm sad when anything dies. A little sad. Not so sad as if there was no chance they might come back, but sad enough. Why are you so interested in Willa, anyway? I'm prettier than she was."

"Oh, I don't know about that. I've seen her photograph. I can't say that I've ever seen a prettier girl than Willa."

"You shut up! She just photographed well is all. And anyway, she's not pretty now. Not anymore. Now she's a dried up old prune at the bottom of a pit, and that's just the right place for her."

"Why, it sounds like you didn't care for Willa at all. What did you have against that child?"

"I've got my reasons for feeling like I do. There's no law that says you have to like every person you know."

"Is that what the angels tell you, Ruth? I'm surprised to hear it."

"I'm not going to speak with you about angels, so you can just keep talking, mister."

"Oh, fine, fine. I was wondering, though. Was Willa so pretty, folks didn't think as much of you?"

"No!" A pause. "You stole her photograph, didn't you? I knew it!"

"It's evidence. Did Clifford Dabney like Willa more than he liked you?"

"That old fool! He doesn't know what he likes."

"He did, didn't he? He liked Willa, and that's why he wanted to come around you lot and spend his money. But then his little friend Willa was gone and yet he kept coming. Now why would he do that? Don't you find that kind of funny, Mrs. Rizzio?"

"I told you not to call me that!"

"Is it funny?"

"It's not funny! He came around because he wanted to bring her back! And because once he knew all about her, we knew he knew all about her, and he wouldn't have wanted anyone else to know that."

"So you and your mother blackmailed him."

"He gave freely."

"I think you have photographs."

It was a shot in the dark, but there were usually cameras present when people did terrible things to one another.

257

"That's true. My mother has the photographs. Disgusting man—he thought he could bring Willa back by lying with her. I don't know where he got such an idea. Certainly not from anything we—anything the angels have written. Maybe he didn't believe it at all, and is just a nasty sort of person."

She shuddered. "I hate him! I hope I never see him again!"

"You won't be so lucky, Mrs. Rizzio. Nor will I."

"Then when I see him, I'm not even going to look at him. He's dead to us now."

"Is that because he ran out of money?"

"He served his usefulness, that's all. People pass through our lives like the rain. Some of them stay a while, others are gone before anyone knows their name."

"How did Willa die, Ruth?"

"I told you—influenza."

"Did you have anything to do with her death?"

"Let's just say I wasn't sorry to see her go."

"Did you help her along?"

"If I did have anything to do with it, nobody knows."

"What did you do—take her blankets off? Wet her down?"

"I'm not telling you! I didn't do anything!"

"Why would you want to hurt a harmless little girl, Miss Ruth? What did she ever do to you?"

"What did she ever do to me? Always so close, watching me with those big eyes, not saying anything. Ever since she was tiny, she followed me around and copied my walk and my voice and the way I do my hair. She was a pest! She'd go up on the altar when she thought nobody was looking and hold the chalice up in her skinny little arms. She stole my old clothes out of the rag bin and made costumes from them. And most everybody thought she was cute—even my mother said so."

"It sounds like you're talking about a little child. Willa was practically a woman."

"I didn't like the child, so why should I care for her when she grew?"

They had reached a sort of impasse.

"What about when you were a child? Have you always lived like this?" He gestured around the opulent chamber.

She was pleased to be asked about herself, and her whole spirit seemed to grow lighter.

"All I've ever known is temples and prayer. My mother had a vision with my birth, Mr. James. It's been my privilege to share that vision, and to help her in the Great Work. There were things I could do that she could not. It's like how children have little fingers, that are more nimble in tying knots. A child's mind is nimble, too. Our dreams are more fluid, easier to slip inside. Mother sent me into the dreamland to bring out messages. She made a home for me where dreams could linger. I expect I've spent as much time in dreams as in what you call the world. I like dreams better."

"Your dreams were nightmares for Sammie, and Frances, and Willa."

"I'm not responsible for them. If they don't like it, they can dream something different."

"How can dead people dream?"

"Their dreams don't die. You're a very stupid man, aren't you?"

"Stupid enough to want to hear you admit you've hurt people—and to hear you tell me why."

She laughed again. She had a pretty laugh.

"Where are you from, Mr. James? Down south some place?"

"Kentucky."

"Well, Kentucky, answer me this. Would you blame a horse for running fast? How about a snake for biting the horse's foot? I was born into this, and all I do is what I've been made for. When my mother birthed me, she saw all the lights from the stars come together into a point that filled the room with heat and light and the most beautiful music she had ever heard. Angels came and told her that we were meant to be together and to make this world more like their world. That's a sacred duty, and no man can speak against it. There are popes and priests and nuns and monks all over the world, doing much the same for their gods. We respect their work. We respect your faith. All we ask is that you respect us, too."

"Respect? But the things you've done are monstrous!"

"That's your opinion. It isn't mine. You asked about Clifford Dabney—"

"What about him?"

"Would it surprise you to know that he was born to be the conduit through which money—money transformed out of oil, transformed out of animal lives long ended—was meant to flow? He was happy while he played this role, happier than you can ever imagine. And Frances? Frances was never more alive than when she lay down her body on the altar of her faith. And what about Ward—you've met Ward, have you not? Do you think anyone else would let that strange little man rise to the heights that he is capable of? He is my mother's husband, Mr. James. That means something. People come to us and make choices. Are we supposed to send them away? To tell them their dreams are lies?"

"All right. But what about Willa? What choices can a little child make about who she lives with or how they treat her?"

"Willa was just like me, though. She was born to die beautiful and believing, and in her death to bind others in

261

shared faith. I would have gladly taken her role—but she's the one who sickened, not me."

"And it was all perfectly natural?"

"What difference does it make? The results are the same. Nobody is upset about this except for you—and you didn't even know her!"

Suddenly furious, he erupted, "They're not the same, because she's lying down at the morgue, covered in the hair of dogs and you're here with your fat ass slipping on satin!"

She briefly gaped, then shut her mouth neatly as her jaw set firm.

"Oh! Oh? Did they give her up, then? That's not good. They won't understand. I guess we'll have to be going soon. What a shame. I kind of liked Los Angeles."

She stood up and shooed him towards the door. "You should leave now. I need to see my mother."

"In a moment. What about Sammie? Was Sammie happy, too?"

She was silent for a moment, and he thought he saw a flash of uncertainty cross her soft face.

"I haven't really thought about Sammie in quite some time. Sammie. Maybe Sammie was a mistake. He wasn't one of us, but I liked him a lot, and wanted to keep him as my pet. He wasn't made to be anybody's pet. He had a mind of his own—a temper. He wasn't suited for this life. I hope he's happier where he is today."

"Where is he today?"

"I'm sure I don't know. He left. That's the truth! Will you go now, Mr. James? You've crashed my world upon the rocks, and I don't expect I have much time before the next wave comes."

He heard a whining in his ears. There were no more questions possible. The house was falling in upon itself and there was no time to waste. He would go and she would pack up her secrets and move on to the next big city, to the next set of victims. Women like Ruth had been absorbing the lives of others since humanity began. She knew her place, as did her victims.

He knew his place, too, as the cool professional seeking answers to satisfy his own curiosity as much as to serve Lady Justice. He didn't really care about Sammie or Frances. And Willa, though so beautiful, had really been no different than Ruth. And maybe he wasn't really so different from Arthur Osborne.

He didn't know what he'd been looking for, but the voices in his head were quiet now. He just wanted to get out of this weird house and back into the sun.

"Good-bye, Miss Ruth. Try not to be too cruel."

She laughed again. She had a pretty laugh. He heard it in his head all the way back home, and sometimes, when he was very tired, for the rest of his life.

Twenty

Down on Broadway, the "Express" boys fussed over their paste-ups, oblivious to the juicy scandal that was coming.

Some stories required massaging before they would inflame the prurient mind, but this one came to them all wrapped up in ribbons.

Two gorgeous girls, one of them freakishly dead. The imposing Mother, with her high hat airs and courtroom outbursts. The corny flock of true believers and their daffy cult monikers. Sexy Ruth's long looks at the jury box. The big Negro who guarded the golden throne and tortured the horses. Missing women. Spurned lovers. Naked dancing. Dirty letters. A murder oven. Angelic voices scribbled on cheap paper. A chance to subtly mock the oilmen who usually soared above their barbs. The boy-husband with his Chinese whiskers and idiot's features. And best of all, the credulous society twerp babbling convoluted nonsense, a perfect clown for dime-stretching citizens who could at least bank on their own good sense.

They played it out over many months in bold headlines, extras and photo features.

"Love Colony Women Hunted—"Angel Gabriel Girls Quizzed"—"Seek New Grave in Cult Probe"—"Cult 'Queen' Tells of Being Chained Two Months to Bed Post"—"'I'm A Dead Man' Was Cult Ritual Cry"—"Cult Leader in Court Row"—"Priestess Snubs Ex-Swain"—"'Divine Music' at Cult Trial"—"Pair Describe Death in Oven"—"Priestess in Collapse at Fraud Trial"—"Sect's Queer Furniture Sold" "Cult Girl's Body Laid in Final Grave."

Mother May was convicted, but the case against her was fatally flawed and she was freed on appeal. There was no law against believing you could commune with holy beings, or talking about it, or fraternizing with others who wished to believe.

"The wonder," mused the judge, "is that rational minds should have become obsessed by such chimerical illusions."

The little group returned to Harmony Hamlet but they kept to themselves. Already wealthy, and scared by their experience, May and Ruth retired from business life. If the Sixth Seal was ever completed, they didn't share its secrets

with outsiders. The tabloids moved on to the next nine days'
wonder. The Great Eleven was forgotten.

But all of that was yet to come. Back in his office, Ray
read over the memo one last time. It was a good one, precise but with more than a hint of poetry. He introduced
the theme of spirituality and the West, circled around the
rivalry and respect between generations, then laid out the
specifics of how young Dabney had come, over the course of
five scant years, to transfer the bulk of his inheritance, his
wife's holdings, and his own modest real estate income into
the hands of May Blackburn and her brood. Inset between
certain transactions, underlined and in capitals, were the
dates and brief descriptions of probable crimes: fraud, the
concealment of a death—probably natural—and the desec-
ration of a corpse.

It was, he thought, enough for the District Attorney to
begin leaning on May Blackburn, in the hopes of extract-
ing certain real property from her possession and driving
her off to the next wide open town, the next cast of suckers.
She wouldn't want to stay, not with the eye of law now upon
her. He marveled again at just how much money had been
melted away on ice for Willa's aboveground grave site, on
animal sacrifice, printed nonsense, and food for an idle cast
of dozens.

The switchboard girl didn't pick up. The old man couldn't still be in his meeting. Memo in hand, he knocked on the heavy door, heard the buzzer, then entered.

Joseph Dabney was sitting in his big leather chair. Across the desk, District Attorney Fitts grunted a greeting.

"Oh, you're here, Chandler. Good, good. That girl of yours really is marvelous, as you keep telling me. Give her a raise, Chandler—not so big as she gets conceited, but a nice little raise."

It was all he could do, but he smiled. "Yes sir."

"Buron is very impressed, very impressed indeed. Isn't that so?" He slammed his fist down on Muriel's memo, the onion skin paper crumpling round his hand.

Fitts nodded and pursed his lips, a hungry look that was the bane of the region's unconnected bad men. Different to others who had occupied his office, he took pleasure in punishment.

"My nephew has really been very lucky, considering. It's a terrible story, a weird one. I don't know how he kept it from me for so long. He's like his mother. The silly child."

Fitts stood. "I'm off, Dabney. You have your attorney file that civil thing in Ventura, and I'll speak with the Sheriff about making sure we get everybody off that mountain. I'll be in touch.

Thanks for the legwork, Chandler—"

And as he passed, he held up the crumpled paper.

Chandler read "from: R. T. Chandler with additional reporting by Muriel Fischer." His heart sputtered and contracted. The cigars and brandy came out, and something like camaraderie with the old man. And as soon as he could, he escaped to Muriel's old room at the Mayfair, where he drank himself into a long, dark hole. When he woke up, he was sore and sick all over, and desperately wished he was at home, wrapped in soft quilts with a hot cup of honey water in his hands. He remembered his promise to Muriel, and he went there, without expectation, but with a willingness to try.

Cissy was kind to him, and he was grateful.

It was the beginning of September, 1929, and the bright soap bubble of American progress was still glinting with rainbows of reflected dreams. They were no realer than Dabney's dreams of eternal life and riches unimagined, and they too would be dashed, spectacularly, soon enough. But for now, the two lovers clung to each other in the dark in their little apartment, feeling the heat of their bodies and the sun's reflected energies oozing from the walls. There was nothing left to try but loving one another, and so they did.

THE END

Subscribers to The Kept Girl

Trudy Penland

Frank Gallagher

Joan Winchell

Lynn Peril

David Smay

Gordon Pattison

Nancy Studhalter

Michael Fijolek

Barbara & Harry Cooper

David Hillary

Joe Pastore

Martha Gruft

Kathleen T. McNeil & Eavan L. McNeil

Charles & Lisa Simon

Joseph Savitz

Barbara Klein & Paul Macirowski

Andrea Canfield

Andy & Nicole Bautista

Joan Renner & Scott Holderman

Diana Parker

UCLA Library of Special Collections

Norman & Roberta Goldberg

Mark Kingwell

Dakota Donovan

Beth Andrus & Art Becerra

Elaine R. Clark & Peter S. Clark

Lanna Pian

Justin & Kathryn Doring

The Huntington Library

Paul Bauer

Patrick Lee

Loren Latker

David Warner

Ruth Waytz & Simon Barsinister

Dwain Carlo Crum

Rodney Hatley

Andrew Gledhill, Kate Holt
    & J. Scott Smith

Howard Prouty

Nicholas Matonak

Adrienne Crew

Ron Tatsui

Jerry & Mary Joseph

Alice Boone

Mark Popham

David Graham

David Rodriguez

David Klappholz & Lisa Klappholz

Thomas Wood

Nathan Marsak

Sybil Davis

Lisa Mayer & E. Sarah Mayer

Carol Hoffstedt

Alicia Bay Laurel

Paul Whitaker & Alicia Whitaker

Tiffany Steffens

Timothy Doherty

Federico Kurschinski

Jon Gallagher & Marian Gallagher

Brad Smith & Dianne Woods

Chris Burlingame

Brett Nair

Hugh & Kathleen McBride

David Hirmes

Mike Towry & Wendy Wildey

Kim Berman

A NOTE ON THE TYPE IN WHICH
THIS BOOK IS SET

This book was designed using the LuaLaTeX typesetting system, and the memoir class written by Peter Wilson. It is set in Bodoni Becker. It is inspired by the 1945 Alfred A. Knopf tenth printing of James M. Cain's "The Postman Always Rings Twice." The type is so called after Giambattista Bodoni (1740-1813), son of a printer of Piedmont. After gaining experience and fame as superintendent of the Press of the Propaganda in Rome, Bodoni became in 1766 the head of the ducal printing house at Parma, which he soon made the foremost of its kind in Europe. His "Manuale Tipografico," completed by his widow in 1818, contains 279 pages of specimens of types, including alphabets of about thirty foreign languages. His editions of Greek, Latin, Italian and French classics, especially his Homer, are celebrated for their typography. In type-designing, he was an innovator, making his new faces rounder, wider and lighter, with greater openness and delicacy. His types were rather too rigidly perfect in detail, the thick lines contrasting sharply with the thin, wiry lines. It was this feature, doubtless, that caused William Morris's condemnation of the Bodoni types as "swelteringly hideous." Bodoni Becker is a modern version based, not upon any one of Bodoni's fonts, but upon a composite conception of the Bodoni manner, designed to avoid the details stigmatized as bad by typographical experts and to secure the pleasing and effective results of which the Bodoni types are capable.

Tower-Lee Company
Incorporated